Growing Up in ALAMANCE COUNTY North Carolina

Growing Up in ALAMANCE COUNTY North Carolina

J. RONALD OAKLEY

THE History PRESS

Published by The History Press
Charleston, SC 29403
www.historypress.net

Back cover, inset: Tom Sykes's print of Main Street in Haw River in the 1950s shows the popular Center Theater, Coles Grocery, and the Riverside Café. *Courtesy of Tom Sykes.*

First published 2014

Manufactured in the United States

ISBN 978.1.62619.326.0

Library of Congress CIP data applied for.

CONTENTS

ACKNOWLEDGEMENTS

This book was made possible by the help of many people. Traci Davenport, the director of the Mebane Historical Museum, encouraged me to undertake this work. Gail Knauff and Cathy Wilson, co-directors of the Haw River Historical Museum, gave me access to the museum's storehouse of photos of Haw River and Alamance County. Jerry Peterman, director of the Graham Historical Museum, shared his photos of Graham. Talented photographer Kelly Gauldin scanned close to one hundred images, from which the photos in this book were selected. Walter Boyd and Don Bolden shared some of their photos of Burlington, and Teresa Dallas provided several photos of Freshwater's Grocery and the Freshwater family. Banks Smither, my commissioning editor at The History Press, provided encouragement and helpful advice on the content and preparation of the book. Most of all, my wife, Kathy, provided invaluable assistance in selecting topics and photographs and served as my editor, critic, and proofreader. For these and so many other reasons, I dedicate this book to her.

INTRODUCTION

I grew up in Mebane, North Carolina, a small mill town nestled up against the eastern border of Alamance County and spilling over into Orange County. Before the coming of the Europeans, the Saxapahaw, Occaneechi, and several other Indian tribes had settled in the county, but most had died out or left in the late eighteenth and nineteenth centuries. At one time, perhaps as many as a dozen Indian settlements existed along Alamance's rivers and streams.

A mainly agricultural county with rolling terrain and an ample water supply from the Haw River and numerous small creeks and streams that helped furnish water power for industry, Alamance County was home to several other little mill towns (Haw River, Altamahaw-Ossipee, Swepsonville, Saxapahaw, Alamance, Hopedale, Carolina, Glen Raven, Bellemont, and Snow Camp) and the quiet little college town of Elon. Burlington, Graham, and Mebane were the only incorporated towns in the county. In 1953, the city of Burlington had a population of 24,560, the eleventh-largest city in the state. Graham, which became the county seat when Alamance separated from Orange in 1849, had over 5,026 people in 1953. Unlike the other towns in Alamance County, Graham developed as a trading and government center rather than a textile area. Mebane's population was about 2,000. By 1961, the population of Alamance County had grown to 85,674.

Alamance County's nearly 150 dairy farms made it one of the leading dairy farming counties in the state. Corn, hay, and tobacco were the major crops. The biggest industry in the county was textiles, followed by furniture.

The leading textile products were hosiery, corduroy, draperies, bedspreads, and curtain materials.

One of the leading employers in the county was Burlington Mills, which had been established in the 1920s by J. Spencer Love to manufacture cotton and rayon bedspreads. Over the years, it continued to expand into hosiery and other fields of natural and man-made fibers. By 1953, it had fourteen plants in Burlington and seventy-five plants and 34,000 employees working in several states and four foreign countries. Another major employer was the Western Electric plant in Burlington, which in the early 1950s employed close to 2,900 people engaged in the making of guided missiles and other electronic equipment.

Growing Up in Alamance County, North Carolina is my personal interpretation of the time, people, places, and events recounted herein. I have tried to re-create what it was like growing up in a small southern town between 1941 and 1959. For me, this was a special time to grow up in Mebane and Alamance County. The purpose of this book is to re-create a time and place and way of life common to many people in small towns across America in the 1950s but now gone.

It's difficult today for some readers to realize how small and protected the world of children could be in a small southern town during this era. It was a great time to be a kid. I really felt that I was master of my life—I had so much freedom to grow, and I was free of so many of the fears and dangers faced by today's kids.

We had radio, books, magazines, and motion pictures, but I was nine years old before I saw my first television. We grew up slower than children do today. We often had to use our imaginations to entertain ourselves, and most of us did that very well. It also was a time of wonder, for we hadn't been bombarded with so many pictures and words about the world beyond our families, our houses, our neighborhoods, and our little town.

This memoir is based on several sources, one of which is the countless hours I spent growing up listening to my parents, siblings, cousins, aunts, and uncles telling stories as we sat on the front porch and at many family reunions and celebrations. Another is the knowledge about this time period I gained through thirty-five years of teaching American history at the college level. Still another is my memory, selective and flawed as it might be. It has been corrected and corroborated by several other sources where possible.

I also researched back issues of the *Mebane Enterprise* and the *Burlington Daily Times-News*, high school yearbooks, and articles and books on the social and cultural history of the 1940s and 1950s.

Introduction

Writing a memoir is a risky enterprise, for it involves writing about people I know and love, many of whom will read what I have written about them. For the most part, I have used the real names of places and people. In only a few cases have I resorted to pseudonyms, and only then to protect the living from unnecessary embarrassment and discomfort. I have tried not to embarrass or slight anyone, and I apologize in advance if I have.

Chapter 1

THE LONG ROAD TO CARR STREET (1920s–1941)

My parents met in Mebane, married in Mebane, and lived in Mebane for the rest of their married lives until they died in 1989. But like so many other residents of the town in the early twentieth century, they both came from somewhere else. My mother, Carrie Cheek, was born in Orange County and moved to Mebane in her teens, while my father, Jesse Oakley, was born in Durham and lived in Person County, Burlington, and then Carrboro before eventually winding up in Mebane. Both came from farming families who moved into town to work in textile factories in hopes of escaping the grinding poverty and uncertainty of agricultural life.

My mother came to Mebane around 1916 from the rural community of Buckhorn. Her father, Dave Cheek, bought a house on the corner of Holt and First Streets, right across the street from his job at Durham Hosiery. The Cheeks moved easily into the life of town dwellers. Soon, with three teenage daughters of courting age—Carrie, Nettie, and Mae—the Cheek house became a popular place for young people to gather to talk, flirt, play records on Dave's windup RCA Victrola, make candy, and have ice cream suppers.

My dad started work in the Durham Hosiery mills when his family moved to Carrboro when he was twelve or thirteen years old. Frequent family moves and going to work in the mills at an early age left little time for school. He quit in the fifth grade, probably because the long days in the mill and chores around the house after work left little time or energy for night school.

In the early 1920s, Durham Hosiery sent him to Mebane to help train the fixers at its mill on South First Street. He rented a room from Mrs. Rosa

The author's parents, Jesse and Carrie Oakley, not long after their 1923 marriage. *Courtesy of the author.*

Berry, who lived right across the street from the Cheek house. He quickly moved into the Cheek circle of friends. He and Carrie soon struck up a courtship, and they married on September 9, 1923, when he was twenty-two and she eighteen.

When they married, Mebane was one of several factory towns that had sprung up in Alamance County in the late nineteenth century. Unlike most of the other mill villages in the county, its major industry would be furniture, not textiles. In the 1920s, Highway 70 was built, running from Beaufort on the coast through the Piedmont, the mountains, and into Tennessee. It paralleled the railroad tracks in Mebane, giving the growing town yet another major transportation artery.

Little Mexico

When my parents married, they lived first in two rooms in a boardinghouse near the mill and then in several mill houses belonging to DixieYarn Mill on the south side of town in an area called Little Mexico. There were few if any Mexicans on that side of town, and I don't know how that section acquired that name. The mill cottages in Little Mexico were similar to the mill cottages in which my father had grown up in Burlington and Carrboro—they were small, built close together, and promoted a strong sense of community, like a family.

The Depression years were difficult for my parents, just as they were for millions of families across the nation. They had four children to feed, and my father had a hard time getting steady work. He worked in several mills in the Alamance County area, often on short time, and he hustled to find work wherever he could, including driving a garbage truck or digging trenches for water and sewer lines for the Town of Mebane.

In the 1930s, the Farm Security Administration/Office of War Information sent photographers across the country to document the effects of the Great Depression. Two of the most famous ones, Dorothea Lange (perhaps best

Farmer offering a pig for sale in downtown Mebane during the 1940 Tobacco Festival. *Courtesy of the Library of Congress.*

A merchant sweeping the street in front of his business, 1940. *Courtesy of the Library of Congress.*

known for her photograph *Migrant Mother*) and Marion Post Wolcott, visited Mebane and snapped dozens of memorable photos of the downtown area during the fall tobacco market.

I was born in 1941, while the nation was still suffering from the Depression and on the verge of entering World War II. I was the last of four children. In 1942, my father got a job with Kingsdown, and in October, when I was about eighteen months old, our family was able to move to a company house on 108 Carr Street. This would be where I grew up and where my parents would live for the rest of their lives.

Chapter 2

THE WAR YEARS

On December 7, 1941, not long after we moved to Carr Street, Japan brought the United States into World War II by bombing its naval base at Pearl Harbor, Hawaii. The war would profoundly affect almost every nation in the world and would help to mold the world in which I grew up.

The day after the bombing at Pearl Harbor, dozens of young men from Alamance County showed up early at the enlistment center in Graham to volunteer for military service, repeating a scene occurring at thousands of offices all across the United States. Eventually, some 15 million American men and women would serve in the conflict, over 362,000 of them from North Carolina, including close to 5,000 from Alamance County. Millions of others from North Carolina and across the nation would go to work in defense plants.

Among the many residents from Mebane who fought in the war was Bogous Shue, a hosiery mill worker who fought in six battles in France and Germany and was training for the invasion of Japan when the war ended. When Shue returned home, he kissed the soil at his home, where his wife and three children were waiting.

David Freshwater of Mebane served in the U.S. Navy. On March 1, 1945, he wrote to his parents, "I'm safe and sound. Of course I'd rather be home with you all, but that is impossible right now. This war will be over some sweet day and then all of us will be together again."

Burlington's John Touloupas served in the U.S. Army in India and Burma. After the war, he rejoined the family business in Burlington at Alamance Hot Weiner Lunch, later renamed Zack's.

Young David Freshwater in his navy uniform during World War II. *Courtesy of Teresa Dallas.*

The war effort was widely supported all across the nation. Patriotic parades in Burlington and other towns attracted large crowds. Banks, schools, retail stores, and post offices sold war bonds, often helped by Hollywood celebrities like John Wayne, Jane Wyman, Wild Bill Elliot, and Lon Chaney, who came to nearby Burlington to promote patriotism and the buying of war bonds. People grumbled but put up with shortages and the rationing of automobile tires, gasoline and other petroleum products, sugar, coffee, cheese, butter, and other consumer goods. Detroit stopped making new automobiles altogether in 1942, and people turned more and more to bus and train travel.

The shortage of metal brought a temporary end to the manufacture of metal toys. For one Christmas, my dad made me a wooden rocking horse and a toy wooden wagon with carved horses that moved up and down as the wagon was pushed across the floor. I still have it today.

Governmental and private agencies organized drives to collect scrap metal, rubber, and other items needed for the war effort. Citizens joined the Civil Air Patrol to help watch for enemy planes and participated in blackout drills, practicing covering the windows with quilts or black cloths to keep the light from escaping.

Alamance County was quickly transformed by the war. While many men and women donned military uniforms, thousands of others worked in factories making war goods. White Furniture Company made fifty thousand double-decker beds for the military, and the textile plants in Burlington, Mebane, and smaller towns across the county quickly converted to manufacturing fabrics for uniforms and other items needed by the military branches.

One of the biggest employers was Fairchild Aircraft and Engine Company, located on Graham-Hopedale Road in a former textile building east of Burlington near the city's small airport. Close to 2,500 workers came there from all across the nation, and a new community of apartments sprang up nearby to house them in an area that came to be called Fairchild Heights. The plant built several kinds of planes, including the Fairchild AT-21 plywood training plane, and with so many men in the military, the plant employed many female workers. Fairchild closed in late 1944 as the military switched to four-engine planes, but Firestone took over and made guns for the last few

World War II war bond portfolio. *Courtesy of Mebane Historical Museum.*

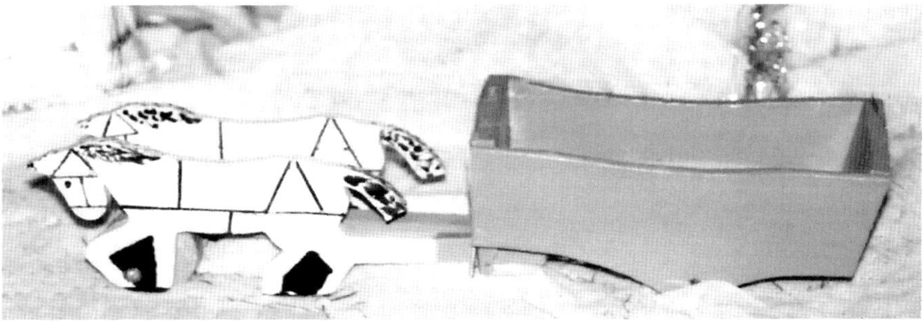

A wooden toy wagon made by the author's father during World War II. *Courtesy of the author.*

months of the conflict. At war's end, Western Electric acquired the factory and continued to do work for the military.

Men and women in uniform were a common sight during the war. A USO center was opened on Davis Street in Burlington to entertain them. Almost every issue of the *Burlington Daily Times-News* and other newspapers carried photographs of young men in service and news of young men killed in action. Many families wondered if and when the father or son(s) would have to go off to war. Young boys in high school worried about being drafted as soon as they graduated, and some quit school to join the military. Three young men on one block in our neighborhood served in the conflict.

If a family had a member in service, they proudly displayed in a window a flag with blue stars. If someone from the family was killed in the war, the flag had gold stars. As the war progressed, so did the number of flags with each color. Men who lost their lives in service were honored at memorial services in churches in their hometowns.

One of my mother's brothers, Vernon Cheek, served in the naval war in the Pacific, and there was some fear my father might be drafted. He had to register with Selective Service in 1943, but his age (forty-three) and four dependent children kept him from being called.

During the war, some 380,000 POWs, mostly German, were shipped to the United States. Close to 10,000 wound up in North Carolina, many of them at Camp Butner, a U.S. Army training camp and hospital in Granville County. Due to labor shortages, POWs were sometimes used to work in the fields of North Carolina farmers. Several worked at the Scott family dairy farm in Alamance County.

Long troop trains, buses, military jeeps, and trucks moved slowly through Mebane carrying men heading for training at Camp Lejeune, Fort Bragg, and other bases down east or on their way to Wilmington to be shipped overseas. As they rode through town, soldiers shouted through the open windows at the crowds that gathered and threw slips of paper with their addresses on them hoping that people would write to them.

Mebane had no USO, but it was a popular social stop for many soldiers, especially those from nearby Camp Butner. They rode the bus to Mebane and went to the Hollywood Movie Theater, a popular refuge from the worries of war until it burned on December 11, 1944. A new theater took its place after the war.

Next door to the theater, the Dollar Soda Shop and bus station functioned in many ways as a USO by providing servicemen a convenient place to play pool, eat hot dogs and sandwiches, and listen to "A String of Pearls,"

"Don't Sit Under the Apple Tree with Anyone Else But Me," and other wartime songs. There the soldiers could meet local teenage girls, who were just as anxious to meet them, since many local boys were in service and were fighting overseas or perhaps sitting in some bus station or soda shop or USO in some other town. The American Legion Hut also held dances for soldiers, providing another site for Mebane girls and soldiers to meet.

I don't remember much about the war, of course, but I do have vague memories of blackouts, soldiers and sailors visiting my sister Velma, and going with my family downtown to join the celebration at the war's end. Velma, who graduated from high school in 1944 and worked part-time at Rose's dime store, often showed up at the bus station, always remembering mother's admonition to watch who she kept company with and to be home no later than 11:00 p.m. She sometimes brought soldiers home to meet Mom and Dad and to have a home-cooked meal. She entertained them in the living room. I soon learned that if I wandered in there, I would be quickly dispatched by a nickel or dime from a lonely soldier trying to buy a little time alone with my big sister. My brother Billy had developed the hobby of collecting military uniform insignias and other memorabilia from the war from soldiers who came to our house. He kept these colorful emblems in a dark green ammunition box given to him by a soldier who was courting Velma.

On Monday, May 7, the *Burlington Daily Times-News* headlined "GERMANY SURRENDERS" and "GREATEST WAR IN ALL HISTORY COMES TO AN END." Atomic bombs were dropped on Japan on August 6 and 9, but still the Asian nation held out. Finally, around seven o'clock on Tuesday night, August 14, President Harry S. Truman announced that Japan had surrendered. The Burlington newspaper rushed out an extra with the headline "JAPANESE ACCEPT TERMS OF ALLIES TO END THE WAR." The newspaper cost five cents.

In cities all across the country, people poured into the streets for celebration parties that lasted far into the night. In Mebane, the fire whistles blew; people ran out into their yards to talk to neighbors; cars paraded through town with their horns honking and passengers waving flags and shouting, "The war is over!" through the windows; people hugged and kissed one another and danced in the streets; and some climbed on the roofs of stores downtown and threw toilet paper and any other kind of paper they could find into the streets.

We went downtown to join in the celebrations. My sisters hopped on a flatbed truck and went to Burlington to join the bigger celebration there. Downtown Burlington was almost paralyzed by a huge traffic jam, and extra policemen had to be called in to control the traffic and the crowds. Governor Robert Gregg Cherry banned the sale of alcoholic beverages, but there were many at these celebrations who managed to find it somewhere. As the *Burlington Daily Times-News* reported on August 15, "Several persons did let their celebration drinking go too far and landed in the lockup for becoming too drunk to handle themselves." The partying in Burlington lasted until daylight Wednesday morning.

Organized victory parades were held in Mebane and Burlington, as in other towns all across the nation. There was more hugging, more dancing in the streets, and a general letting go after four long years of war. In Mebane, as elsewhere, large crowds attended special prayer services at their churches on Wednesday night to give thanks for the end of the war.

One of the songs popular during the war was "When the Lights Come on Again." On August 14, 1945, the lights came on. Rationing soon ended, men came home and resumed their lives, other men who had just been drafted or finished military training learned they would not be going to battle after all, and local plants returned to peacetime production.

But for some, there would be no getting on with their lives. Among the more than 400,000 Americans lost in the war were some 4,000 North Carolinians killed in battle and another 3,000 who died from related causes. Over 200 men and women from Alamance County died in the conflict. Many others suffered physical and mental wounds that healed slowly or never at all.

Chapter 3

HOME SWEET HOME

With the war over, life was happier in our little house on North Carr Street. Cutting off North Highway 119 about a half mile from the center of town, Carr Street was in a working-class neighborhood made up of small frame homes dating back to the 1920s. Most were company houses originally built by local factories and rented to the workers, most of whom worked in one of the three hosiery mills just a block away, at White's Furniture and Kingsdown downtown, or at the two hosiery mills by the railroad. Others worked in mills in Haw River, Swepsonville, and Burlington; retail stores in downtown Mebane; or at Western Electric in Burlington, which was unionized and paid higher wages and benefits than other factories in the county.

In the early 1940s, our Carr Street home was a small six-room frame structure with front and back porches. The small kitchen had a kerosene cookstove, an icebox, a sink, and an adjoining pantry. Ice was delivered every other day by a large black man from the W.D. Sykes Ice and Coal Company, which also delivered coal during the winter. A small, unheated bathroom opened off the back porch. We were lucky—some houses in our neighborhood still had outdoor privies. There was no central heat, so the house was heated by a wood- and coal-burning stove in one bedroom/sitting room and by fireplaces in the living room and second bedroom. Until the late 1940s, my parents kept chickens in the backyard, and until well into the 1970s, they had a small vegetable garden in which they grew corn, tomatoes, peas, and beans for immediate use or canning.

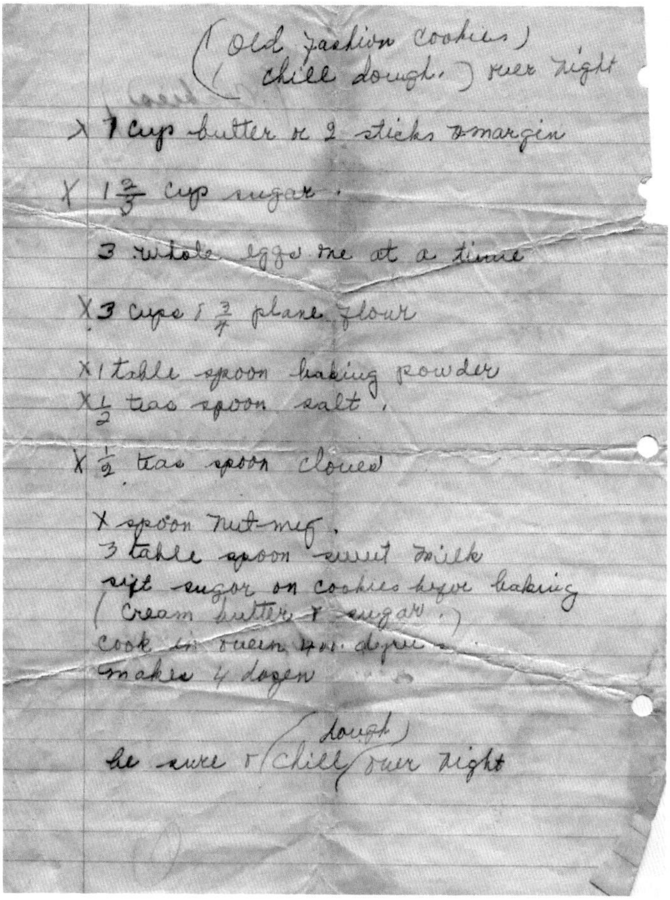

(Old fashion cookies)
(chill dough.) over night

X 1 cup butter or 2 sticks margin

X 1 2/3 cup sugar.

3 whole eggs one at a time

X 3 cups & 3/4 plane flour

X 1 table spoon baking powder
X 1/2 tea spoon salt.

X 1/2 tea spoon cloves

X spoon nut-meg.
3 table spoon sweet milk
sift sugar on cookies before baking
(Cream butter & sugar.)
cook in oven 400 degree
makes 4 dozen

be sure & chill (dough) over night

Mother's cookie recipe. *Courtesy of the author.*

In 1947, my father bought the house for about $4,000 from Kingsdown, which, like many industries, was finding it too expensive and troublesome to build and maintain rental houses for its workers. After close to twenty-five years of renting, my parents finally owned their own place, and now my father employed his handyman skills to update and expand the house and turn it into real home. But we still didn't have central heat, and on cold winter nights we warmed ourselves by a kerosene stove in the den and then ran and jumped into the cold bed wearing socks, sweaters, and even toboggans or ear muffs.

One of my parents' main sources of pride was the living room, which was more like a small, rarely used parlor. It had a sofa, two formal chairs, a fireplace, a coffee table with a glass top, a player piano, built-in shelves on each side of the fireplace, and a standalone bookcase that contained an

The Oakley house on Carr Street, circa 1950. *Courtesy of the author.*

old photo album, a Bible, and a few other books. I don't know where the player piano came from or why we had it because none of us could play it or ever thought of taking lessons so we could. But a piano was a sign of respectability and prosperity, and it was fun to put in one of the paper rolls and see the keys move and hear the music come out automatically—just like a radio! The room was used mainly when company called, when Velma or Colleen had a date, and as a place to put the Christmas tree.

From my early childhood days, I can remember watching my parents making lye soap in a big boiling pot and washing clothes with Octagon Soap on large rippled washboards in big tin tubs in the backyard. I can also remember taking "bird baths" in tin washtubs in warm water that had been heated on the stove and dyeing and hunting for Easter eggs. I will never forget their home remedies—fatback meat to rub on the chiggers we caught when we were playing outside or picking blackberries, castor oil or water enemas for intestinal problems, and mustard plasters for colds and respiratory ailments. The mustard plasters were hot, foul-smelling cloths placed on the chest to supposedly sweat out the offending bacteria or viruses causing us to have sore throats, bronchitis, and related problems. I was so glad when they switched to Vick's VapoRub, manufactured in nearby Greensboro.

D4 Burlington, N.C. Times-News Saturday, September 2, 1995

Octagon Soap is almost as c

By MABLE LASSITER

If you are familiar with the strains of "Wine and Roses," then brush cobwebs away from your store of memories and meditate for a while on Octagon Soap, first made in 1806 and destined to become a household name even into this century.

Though out-dated today, Octagon's history is filled with interesting facts since Colgate and Co. was founded by William Colgate as a starch, soap and candle business in New York City, but the following year the name became Smith and Colgate with Smith being a partner. By 1864 Colgate and Co. was providing soap to the White House, about the time a factory was opened in Milwaukee that in time became the Palmolive Co. Sale of starch was discontinued in 1866, but a short time later the Peet Brothers began a soap company in Kansas City to produce the first milled perfume, Cashmere Bouquet Toilet Soap. Improvements continued to be evident, and by 1906 Palmolive had become a floating soap and Colgate produced numerous soaps, 160 different toilet perfume. One of the company's major contributions came during World War I when a product was developed by Colgate for protection of the body from exposure to poison gas. The present name of the company that began Octagon soap in 1806 is the Colgate Palmolive Co. with the name adopted in 1953.

No other factory in the soap boiling operation was, on such a large scale of producing with mechanical facilities, so perfect. Every advertised improvement, learned from modern chemical science, with the help of the best mechanical engineering, was found there. One of the three great kettles initially used was capable of holding 6,000,000 pounds of Octagon soap. The stock (beef tallow) was purchased at the butcher shop, and it was rendered, strained, and purified so that it was clean and sweet. Under no condition would it ever become rancid.

Octagon contained rosin, an ingredient necessary for perfect cleaning uses. The rosin gave the soap its yellowish color. Rosin is made from the sap of pine trees, much of it The sap is distilled, extracting turpentine and leaving rosin residue.

When the question about the yellowish color of Octagor soap, manufactures stated that the eye may be attracted to white soap but no one could find cleaner, whiter suds than the Octagon. Because boiling clothes was nor mal in the early stages of Octagon soap use, the publicity brochures never failed to include this helpful hint: "It is always best to boil clothes after they've been properly washed to assure a fresher, cleaner wash." The Octagon bar itself was formed by pre sure into a solid condensed piece with no air holes.

Another suggestion the company extended its custo ers was: "Only a trace of bl ing is necessary, and since Octogan leaves clothes clea and white, the bluing proc may be left out entirely du ing this time of the year." fore the days of modern d ers, Octagon offered these timely hints to housewive "A gentle breeze and not much sun is the best con tion for drying clothes. D put clothes on bushes or es due to their being du

Octagon Soap, a popular general-purpose soap. *Courtesy of the Mebane Historical Museum.*

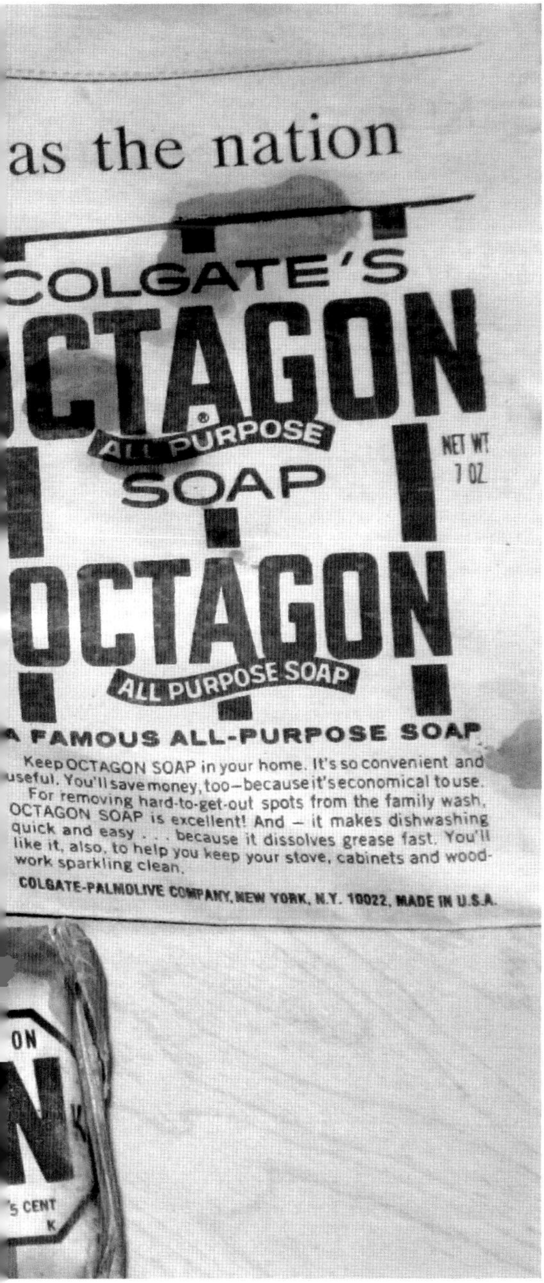

It was a time when people didn't call before they came to visit but simply showed up, expecting to find you at home. Since we rarely locked our doors before bedtime, they sometimes just walked in saying, "Carrie and Jesse, you've got company."

The Neighborhood

Our closest neighbors were Gurdy and Alphadene Harris. Their son, James, his wife Marie and their two children (Judy and Jimmy) lived in the house with them. Alphadene was a short, plump, delightful little woman I always called "Harrisy." She was Mother's best friend for many years.

Diagonally across the street from us in a two-story brick home lived Emma Harris and her housekeeper, Georgia Bradley. Miss Emma, as most people called her, was rich by Mebane standards. A spinster, she centered her life around her church, civic activities, and her flower gardens and garden club. When you went by her house, you often saw her dressed in overalls and old shoes, digging, shoveling and pruning in her flower beds. Some people thought it was a little strange for a woman to dress and work so much like a man, but Miss Emma didn't care what people thought.

She was hard of hearing, making it very difficult to talk with her. It also made it hard for her to drive, for she couldn't hear the car motor running. When she started her old car in her garage, she pushed the accelerator way down while it warmed up, and she seemed to have trouble manipulating the clutch and the accelerator as the car shot out of the driveway. Other motorists and pedestrians always scrambled to get out of her way when they heard her coming down the street on her way to church or her garden club meeting or wherever she was going.

Mebane native Edwin Yoder Jr., a Pulitzer Prize–winning journalist and son of the high school principal, later wrote in *The Night of the Old South Ball and Other Essays and Fables* that when Miss Emma left the Presbyterian Church on Sunday at noon, "traffic parted to make way, like the Red Sea before the Children of Israel."

The neighborhood was like an extended family. Everybody knew everybody, really meant it when they asked how you were doing, and looked after one another's children if they were playing in their yard. In times of sickness, people visited and brought food, and when someone in the neighborhood died, took up money for flowers from other neighbors. Sometimes Harrisy would come in the back door and sit for a while and talk with Mother while she cooked or washed dishes.

The Clothesline

In this close, friendly neighborhood, women met and talked across the clothesline as they hung out the day's laundry in the backyard. The conversation covered a broad spectrum—children, relatives, medical problems, marital problems, the weather, and local gossip. Mother hung out clothes several mornings a week, usually timing it so that Harrisy would be hanging hers out, too, and they could talk.

The items dangling from clotheslines told the neighbors and passersby a lot about the occupants of the house. You didn't have to be Perry Mason to discern the significance of diapers, teenage bathing suits, short underwear and long johns with a buttoned flap on the back, bras, clothing with holes, and work uniforms. Sometimes summer thunderstorms drenched the clothes before they could be gathered in, dogs pulled pants off the line and chewed them, and birds occasionally made a deposit.

Sitting on the Porch

During warm months, it was a neighborhood of porch-sitters. Front porches provided relief from the summer heat—especially in working-class neighborhoods like ours—and took you close to the sounds and smells of the outdoors. Porch-sitting could be done anytime during warm weather, but it was best in the late afternoon and evenings when the sun went down, the light faded, and the air began to cool. Up and down our street, the neighborhood came alive after supper as families headed to the porch to cool off before going to bed. We usually cut the lights off inside the house so that we could enjoy the dusk and darkness as we sat in rocking chairs or the swing.

Sipping sweet iced tea or a Coca-Cola, we used this time to unwind from the day's work or play, talk over the day's events, discuss individual and family problems, gossip about the neighbors, and pass on family stories dating back decades. Sometimes my father relaxed by smoking king-sized Chesterfields while my mother snapped beans, shucked corn, or darned socks.

The Oakley family on the front porch of their home in the mid-1940s. *Courtesy of the author.*

Jesse Oakley relaxing on the front porch with a Chesterfield. *Courtesy of the author.*

The front porch was our window to the little world of Carr Street and the wider world of Mebane. From our front porch, we had a clear view of the neighborhood and the street in front of our house. Children played games or chased lightning bugs in the yards or street under the watchful eyes of adults. Neighbors waved to one another and often dropped by to chat. Everybody knew everybody else, and if a stranger walked down the street, all eyes on every porch followed his passing as people whispered, "Now, who is he, and what is he up to?"

The porch made us accessible to friends and acquaintances who often waved or exchanged greetings as they walked by or slowly drove by. Sometimes they stopped and came up to our porch to sit, enjoy a cold soft drink or iced tea, and talk about anything from the weather and politics to the recent surgery or death of a friend. The porch offered a convenient way to entertain without having to invite guests, particularly casual acquaintances, inside the house. Over the years, we talked to far more people on the porch than ever came inside our house.

Our porch had often been a favorite place for courting. My sisters had entertained dates on our porch, but by the time I started dating in the mid-1950s, the courting tradition on front porches was being replaced by automobiles, which offered more privacy and mobility and, as some people said, put sex on wheels.

Door-to-Door Salesmen

Door-to-door salesmen were common in our neighborhood at a time when people weren't afraid to let them in the house. In the summer, my parents bought fresh vegetables from local farmers, black and white, who came through the neighborhood selling produce from the trunks of their cars or the backs of their pickup trucks. Some of them came year after year and became familiar visitors to the neighborhood.

Some of our neighbors had dairy products delivered to their porch by Melville Dairy, located in Burlington, but we purchased ours from a local

A Melville Dairy Truck in the 1950s. *Courtesy of the Scott Collection.*

farmer, Henry Heath, who for years showed up every Saturday afternoon in his old Model A Ford with fresh milk, buttermilk, butter, and eggs. He always took time to talk about the weather, his aches and pains, his children, and the children of his customers. To this day, I've never tasted better buttermilk than that delivered by the wizened little man everyone called Mr. Henry.

Besides Mr. Henry and other farmers who came around selling their products, we had Jehovah's Witnesses and other religious groups peddling their brands of religion, traveling Bible and magazine subscription salesmen, Electrolux vacuum cleaner vendors, Fuller Brush vendors selling all kinds of brushes and cleaning products, and a Jewel Tea salesman.

The Jewel Tea salesman traveled in a paneled truck, a far cry from the turn of the century, when the company sold coffee and tea from the back of a horse-drawn wagon. When he came through our neighborhood in the 1950s, he displayed samples of popcorn, peanut butter, mayonnaise, soap, cooking pots and pans, and dozens of other items, and he took orders to be delivered later. Mother thought his prices were too high and rarely bought from him, but she usually let him in the house to make his sales pitch.

The Help

Carr Street was a white world except for black domestic workers who came into the neighborhood in the morning and left in the afternoon, Monday through Friday. Saturday was sometimes a day when black people came to help with house cleaning, yard work, and other special projects.

Several people in our neighborhood and in white neighborhoods all across town hired black women to keep their children and cook and clean while they were at work. For several hours each day, these female domestics lived in intimate relationships with their white employers and then went home to what were usually less desirable living situations. This was a common practice all across the South during these Jim Crow days, and most of us rarely questioned it. They were usually called by their first names—Annie, Willie May, Daisy, Lillian—and I never knew their last names.

For several years after my birth, Mother and Daddy hired a large, jovial black woman named Alice to come in occasionally to help with the cooking and cleaning during the busy times of Thanksgiving, Christmas, and spring cleaning. She came frequently when Mother was experiencing headaches and other discomforts during menopause.

Alice walked or hitched a ride from her house in the black section off of Highway 70 south of town. Sometimes she brought her two young children, Jerry and Jean. I was always fascinated by these visitors who looked and talked so different from everyone else I knew, and I always looked forward to their visits. Alice loved to tease me, and Jerry and Jean were two more playmates for me to enjoy. I never really questioned why they came to our house and why they sat down and ate the lunch Alice had prepared only *after* we had finished eating.

Some whites who hired blacks to work for them inside their houses were always worried about their cleanliness and their honesty. Many were afraid that they would "catch" something from the domestics who lived in their homes several hours each day, sitting on their chairs or sofas and using their bathroom, dishes and silverware. Many were also worried about their domestics stealing money, jewelry, clothing, and other valuables while they were off at work. Yet they trusted them to look after their children and to prepare supper for the family at the end of the day.

Chapter 4

FRESHWATER'S AND OTHER NEIGHBORHOOD GROCERY STORES

In the era before the prevalence of large chain grocery stores and supermarkets, Alamance County was blessed with numerous locally owned and operated grocery stores that also doubled as social centers for the neighborhood, friendly places where people came not just to buy groceries or snacks but also to catch up on the latest neighborhood news or gossip, share their sometimes passionate opinions about politics, argue about the latest college or high school football or basketball game, play cards or checkers, or share the latest joke they had heard. The stores were also places to take up money to send flowers to a neighbor who had a sickness or death in the family.

Some of the stores were located in the countryside not far from town. One of the most popular was the Stainback General Store, located just a few miles outside of Mebane near Crossroads Presbyterian Church. Opened in 1881, the store was run by several generations of the Stainback family until it closed in the early 1960s. Over the years, the store was the hub of the rural community, operating a post office and photography studio, providing a public telephone, serving as a place for the dissemination of information, and selling just about everything the community needed, from groceries to caskets. Today, the store is on the National Register of Historic Places and is owned by the Mebane Historical Society.

Downtown Mebane had several stores. One of the most popular ones was the R.T. Dunn Grocery on Clay Street. My father often shopped there

Above: R.T. Dunn's store in downtown Mebane. *Courtesy of Florene Dunn.*

Left: Thad Freshwater in front of his store in the 1940s. *Courtesy of Teresa Dallas.*

because he was a close friend of the owner and because the store specialized in a variety of fresh-cut meats.

About a block from our house was my family's favorite store and the social center of our neighborhood, David Freshwater's Grocery, located on the corner of Highway 119 and West Crawford Street. It was the oldest business in Mebane operating under one name at the same location. It dated back to 1914, when David's father, Thad, opened it when Highway 119 was just a dirt road, an old stagecoach trail.

When Thad died in 1946, David, who had worked in the store for much of his life except when he served in the navy during World War II, took over the running of the store. Like his parents, he and his family lived in a two-story house behind the store for several years.

Going to David's was always an adventure, and I went at least once every day, sometimes more often in the summertime when school was

Elma and David Freshwater pose behind Freshwater's Grocery. *Courtesy of Teresa Dallas.*

Front of Freshwater's Grocery in summertime. *Courtesy of author.*

out. Like so many of his customers, we had a charge account that my father settled up on payday. He allowed me to charge ten cents a day, enough for a soft drink and a candy bar or pack of peanuts. Sometimes I went to the store for one of our neighbors, Miss Emma Harris, and her housekeeper, Miss Georgia Bradley, who would telephone and ask me to go to the store for her, usually to get one or two small items like sewing thread or Railroad Mills Snuff. Sometimes she rewarded me with a nickel, and sometimes she didn't.

The store sat so close to the highway that a car could barely park between the front porch and the road. The little porch was usually loaded down with fresh watermelons, cantaloupes, corn, and tomatoes in the summer and baskets of apples and pumpkins in the fall. It creaked with every step you took, as did the floor inside.

Standing and reigning over the small store from behind a counter facing the front door, David greeted every customer who came in. An adding machine, scales, charge pads, a hoop of cheese, and a roll of white paper used for wrapping slices of fatback or cheese sat on the counter, and underneath the counter was a wooden drawer with hollowed-out bins for different denominations of change and bills. Below the drawer was a large shelf that held slabs of fatback meat. He never sold beer because he wanted the store to be a family place.

Freshwater's never had a telephone, modern cash register, or bathroom. David added the figures in his head or on an old adding machine and wrote down charged purchases in a green hardbound account book.

Behind David was an easy chair beside a woodstove, and to his right along the wall were a couple of old straight-backed chairs and a large (110-pound) empty Jewel Lard can that also served as a chair, though not a very comfortable one. In the winter, I loved to sit around the stove and talk to David and others who came in the store. I couldn't always get a seat, though, because others from the neighborhood also came to sit and talk to David and to other customers who walked up to the counter to pay for their goods or to ask David to slice them a hunk of cheese or a pound of fatback. Some regulars even brought their own chairs, and on one occasion, one of the men had a falling out with the others and took his chair home and did not return for several months.

Near the front was my favorite part of the store—the glass candy case with only sliding doors between me and Sugar Daddies, Baby Ruths, Hersheys, Mary Janes, B-B-Bats, Butterfingers, and other delicacies. Boxes of Cracker Jacks were usually stacked on top of the case along with bags of Red Bird Peppermint Sticks and several varieties of packaged peanut butter and cheese crackers. An ice cream box also sat near the front window, filled with Brown Mule popsicles, Dreamsicles, pints and small cups of ice cream, and ice cream sandwiches. The choices were tantalizing and seemingly endless.

David was a large, good-humored man in his twenties and thirties when I frequented the store when I was growing up. He joked with all his customers, including kids like me, and never ran out of patience as he stood behind the candy counter while I tried to decide what kind of candy I wanted that day. When he gave change back, he sometimes flipped one of the coins in the air and caught it behind his back or after he bounced it on the counter.

After playing baseball or football, my friends and I would ride our bikes to the store, where we sat around inside or on the porch drinking soft drinks and eating peanuts and candy bars. Sometimes eight or ten of us would be gathered around the porch at one time. If it ever bothered David, he never said anything about it.

Freshwater's was one of the most popular grocery stores in town, drawing customers not just from the neighborhood but from the entire town of Mebane and other nearby towns as well. His customers came from all walks of life—townspeople, black and white farmers from outlying areas, local housewives who walked or drove to pick up a few items, or kids like me who walked or rode our bicycles. Many farmers, both black and white, charged their groceries for months at a time and then paid up when they sold their tobacco or other crops. Customers stood around talking with the postman or businessmen or sat around the stove talking or even on the porch. Workers from the two nearby hosiery mills came over at break time or lunch time and sat on the porch or inside talking and eating crackers or sandwiches. For many years, T.D. Jones and Bill Warren coordinated their mail delivery routes so they could arrive at the store to have lunch together.

The store was a magical place at Christmas, when it was so packed with seasonal products that you could hardly walk down the center aisle to the counter. There would be bags of apples and oranges, nuts of all kinds, coconuts, Christmas candy and cider, and country hams and bags of peanuts hanging on wire dangling from the ceiling. It *looked* and *smelled* like Christmas.

We bought most of our groceries there, as did many of David's customers, choosing them from shelves and tables whose arrangement and location changed very little over the years. When my dad was injured in 1950 and stayed out of work for many months, David let him run up a large tab and

The author, with two Coca-Colas in hand, enjoys refreshments at the grand opening of the Colonial Store in the late 1950s. *Courtesy of the author.*

sometimes even delivered groceries after he closed at night. In the late 1980s, when my aging parents were failing rapidly, he took groceries by their house, including a carton of my father's beloved bottled Coca-Colas and Chesterfield cigarettes.

Freshwater's store was one of a dying breed at mid-century. In the mid-1950s, the Colonial Store, Byrd's, and other chain food stores moved into Mebane, Graham, and Burlington. Soon some of David's customers defected to the chains, lured by their wider selections and cheaper prices. His customers were not just customers but also friends, and it was awkward for them and for David when they visited his store less often or stopped coming at all. Some still came, mainly for the fresh produce that David provided.

David knew he couldn't compete with the supermarkets in canned goods and other prepackaged items, so he carved out his own niche by providing personal service and stocking fresh meats and produce that were cheaper and fresher than what the chains carried. For decades, he got up at 4:00 a.m. and drove the fifty miles to the farmer's market in Winston-Salem to buy fresh produce and then returned home in time to open the store at 7:00 a.m. It was a hard life, but he managed to survive while most other small grocery stores around town disappeared.

Under both Mr. Thad and David, this little corner store was the center of the neighborhood for decades, and it would continue to be so until early in the third millennium.

Chapter 5
ENTERTAINMENT

The Radio

Entertainment in our home centered on the radio and, from the early 1950s on, television. The first commercial radio station in the United States went on the air in Pittsburgh in 1920, and when my parents married in 1923, this new marvel was still fairly expensive for mill-working families like ours. It brought a whole new world into their little rented house.

The radio connected them to the outside world, to the world of popular songs, professional boxing, comedies, dramas, and news of current events. When I came along, radio was in its golden age, and my mother kept it on for much of the day as she did her ironing, cleaning, cooking, and other chores. It was usually tuned to WFFN in Burlington, especially during the hours when guitar player Texas Jim Hall was on the air playing the music of Ernest Tubb, Little Jimmy Dickens, Hank Williams, and other hillbilly and country music stars.

Hall and his Radio Rangers recorded their own songs and performed at barn dances in Burlington, Greensboro, and other local towns, and sometimes at the Veterans Hospital near Durham. He also used his radio show as a fundraiser for the March of Dimes and other charitable causes.

Every Saturday night from 7:30 until midnight, the radio was likely to be tuned to WSM for the live performance from Nashville of *The Grand Ole Opry*, the mecca of country music, featuring Minnie Pearl and other popular performers.

The Fan Club of 'JIM HALL' and His Radio Rangers . . .
(Good Luck—Good Cheer—Good Deed—Friendship Club.)
Blue Ribbon Record Star - - - - - - Song Writer)

— presents —

JIM HALL NEWS

Our First Issue | 1951 | May, June, July, Aug.

Boost Blue Ribbon Records by JIM HALL: The Flivver Song Waitin in Ole Caroline . . . first Blue Ribbon records

WE HONOR

JIM HALL

ASK FOR
"JIM HALL"
ON
BLUE RIBBON
RECORDS

LATEST
The Flivver Song
Waiting in ole Caroline

BOOST *Our Star* *and* *Records*

Newsletter of popular Burlington radio personality Jim Hall. *Courtesy of the Haw River Historical Museum.*

When Velma, Colleen, or Billy had control of the dial, it was usually turned to the swing and big-band music of the war and postwar era, the Andrews Sisters, Frank Sinatra, Bing Crosby, and other crooners with familiar names and voices at our house. With few exceptions, like Gene Autry's 1949 hit "Rudolph the Red-Nosed Reindeer," there was no separate popular music for children or teenagers until I entered my teenage years and was captivated by rock-and-roll. Before then, I heard and liked what my parents and siblings liked, and I heard it on the radio. We didn't have a record player.

On Saturday and Sunday nights, we gathered around our Philco console in the living room to listen to the popular programs of the day. We rarely ever missed the shows of Phil Harris and Alice Faye, Jack Benny, Fred Allen, George Burns and Gracie Allen, Edgar Bergen and Charlie McCarthy, or Amos and Andy.

I had favorite shows I listened to in the late afternoon, sitting by the radio in the den, especially on cold, rainy winter afternoons unsuitable for outdoor play. I enjoyed *Bobby Benson and the B-Bar-B Riders* and *Sergeant Preston of the Yukon*, but the show I didn't dare miss was *The Lone Ranger*. Every Monday, Wednesday, and Friday afternoon at five o'clock, I listened to the adventures of the masked man and his loyal Indian sidekick, Tonto. The show began with a few bars from the "William Tell Overture," gunshots, hoof beats and the dramatic announcement, "A fiery horse with the speed of light…Return with us now to those thrilling days of yesteryear…."

It didn't bother me that Tonto's sentences contained a mixture of good English, problems with pronouns ("Me go circle to the back of the shooters"), and a good deal of grunting. I didn't find it strange that the Lone Ranger sometimes talked to his horse: "Hi-yo, Silver—awa-a-a-a-ay!" and "Silver, we've got to head over to the ranch" and "Let's go, big fellow." After all, a lot of cowboys on the radio and in the movies talked to their horses. He wore a mask to conceal his identity and had a high moral code, and I always knew that the show would end with justice being done and the Lone Ranger and his Indian sidekick riding off after their successful mission and someone saying, "Who was that masked man, anyway?" and then being told, "Why, don't you know? That was the Lone Ranger."

I was really into it. I had two Lone Ranger cap pistols and holsters, and I joined the Lone Ranger Club, which allowed me to send off the seal on Merita Bread wrappers for a silver bullet (which doubled as a pencil sharpener), a mask, a card with the Ranger's secret code, and other paraphernalia.

The Mebane Theater

Long before television came into our lives on Carr Street, there was the Mebane Theater, one of several movie theaters in Alamance County. In my early years, it was truly a magical house of entertainment and a window to the world outside of Mebane.

The theater was a two-story structure on Center Street next to the post office and across the street from the railroad tracks and Kingsdown. As a child, I first paid nine cents for admission and then, later, fifteen cents. Then, when I was a teenager, I believe it went to thirty-five and then fifty cents. For years, I could get a complete entertainment package for only thirty-five cents—fifteen cents to get in, ten cents for popcorn and five cents for a soft drink, candy bar, or a box of delicious Goobers Chocolate Covered Peanuts.

The aisles and spaces between the rows of seats were always sticky from years of spilled soft drinks, candy, and buttered popcorn. Rarely a night went by when the movie wasn't interrupted when the film broke and we'd have to patiently sit in the dark while it was being fixed.

Only whites could sit downstairs in the main seating area. Blacks entered through a separate outside entrance and sat in the balcony. That was just the way it was, and until I reached my mid-teens, I never really wondered why it was that way. Sometimes I went to the theater with family members or other boys in the neighborhood, and in my teens, I sometimes met a girl there and held her hand during the movie. We never necked—that would have to wait until later years at the drive-in theater in Burlington.

When I was a child, my favorite day to go to the theater was Saturday, when it opened at eleven o'clock in the morning and remained open until the end of the last feature at night. There was always a double feature, including at least one western, a cartoon, the *News of the Day*, and a serial, such as *Superman* or *Batman*, that ended with a cliffhanger designed to bring you back to the theater the next Saturday. I didn't care much for the newsreels, for I knew little about the Korean War, McCarthyism, Ike, or Truman. Basically, I just wanted to get through them and on to the cartoons and main attraction.

The first movie I remember seeing was Walt Disney's animated musical film *Song of the South*. My father took me to see it, and he seemed to like it as much as I did. I also saw *Gone with the Wind* several times, as did many other southerners. These two movies formed my views on southern history for years to come.

As an adolescent and young teenager, I saw many films at the Mebane Theater: vintage World War II films that ended with the message to "Buy

War Bonds," Rogers and Hammerstein musicals, cops-and-robbers films, comedies (Dean Martin and Jerry Lewis and the Bowery Boys), *The Ten Commandments* and other films loosely based on the Bible, and science fiction films about space wars, alien invasions, the dangers of radiation, monsters from beneath the sea, giant lizards, and, most memorably, *The Thing from Another World*. In 1952, trying to compete with television and reverse declines at the box office, Hollywood came out with *Bwana Devil* and *House of Wax*, but I didn't think that the illusion of having spears appear to come straight out into the audience was worth the ten cents I had to pay for the special 3-D glasses. I didn't bother to see the other 3-D films that came to Mebane during Hollywood's brief experiment with them.

For several years during my childhood, my favorite movies were the B-grade cowboy films I saw every Saturday morning sitting in the dark theater wearing my cowboy hat and boots and my Lone Ranger cap pistols strapped to my waist. It didn't matter who it was—Roy Rogers and his faithful horse Trigger, his wife, Dale, and his sidekick, Gabby Hayes; Gene Autry and his equally faithful horse Champion; or Hopalong Cassidy on his white horse Topper.

I don't remember being concerned about the fact that the cowboys didn't have gainful employment, that even though they were cowboys they really didn't own any cows, and that Roy and Gene sometimes broke into song (Rogers even had a band, the Sons of the Pioneers) out in the middle of the wilderness. What really mattered was that they were the good guys, the defenders of women and children and decent families and others in need, avengers of wrongs, the good guys out to defeat those who weren't. They were men of honor who lived by the cowboy code of the Old West; they never cursed, never drank anything stronger than milk, always kept their word, always fought fair against bad guys who didn't, respected women and the elderly, and always caught the bad guys—the bank and train robbers, cattle rustlers, and other lawbreakers. The good guys never killed anyone; instead, they shot the gun out of their hand, wounded them in the arm or leg, or lassoed them and tied them up. Then there were Lash LaRue and Whip Wilson, who used whips along with their guns to get the best of the bad guys. Both could use their bullwhip to snatch a gun or knife out of a bad guy's hand as fast as the blink of an eye. A cut above these B-grade horse operas were the western movies of Randolph Scott, John Wayne, Gary Cooper, and Alan Ladd. Some of their movies were in Technicolor.

The Mebane Theater was a popular place until television came along with its siren song to stay home and be entertained for free. People stood in long lines with dates or family to see the latest films. Many people walked to and from the theater, often stopping by one of the three nearby drugstores before or afterward for ice cream or milkshakes or going by Betty's Snack Shack for hot dogs or hamburgers. After we left the Mebane Theater, we usually stopped at Betty's Snack Shack—even late at night—for hot dogs and French fries. You could smell them as you walked out of the theater, and it was impossible to walk by the little shop without stopping. The owner and his employees would hand you your hot dogs and take your money through a small window. Blacks and whites stopped by and, by custom, segregated themselves—the blacks sat on benches on one side and the whites on the other.

As we got older, we sometimes went to see movies in Graham or Burlington. Burlington had three movie theaters, each one much larger than the Mebane Theater. In the early 1950s, they installed air conditioning and

Popular western movie star Hopalong Cassidy promoting Melville Dairy in Burlington. *Courtesy of the Scott Collection.*

tried to lure customers with door or marquee signs announcing, "It's Cool Inside." At the Carolina Theater, black patrons had to enter by a side door and sit in the balcony.

In this heyday of the B-grade westerns, Hopalong Cassidy (William Boyd), Hoot Gibson, Sunset Carson, and several other stars made public appearances at these theaters to promote their movies, local charitable causes, and commercial products that they sponsored. Cassidy, a popular spokesman for Melville Dairy, appeared before signs urging kids to drink milk so they could "be big and strong like Hopalong." He sometimes rode his horse Topper in Burlington's Christmas parades.

In the 1940s and '50s, it seemed that everybody loved a parade—patriotic parades during and at the end of World War II; the annual Tobacco Festival Parade in Mebane; the 1949 Alamance County Centennial Celebration parades in Burlington, Graham and Mebane; and the annual Christmas parades in several towns. The Jordan Sellers High School Marching Band from the all-black Burlington school was a popular attraction in many parades in the county. Evening street dances also drew large crowds in Mebane, Burlington, Graham, and other Alamance County towns.

Television

In the early 1950s, our home was transformed when we got a magic box for our living room. In July 1949, Charlotte became the first city in the state to have a television station (WBTV), and it was followed just a few weeks later in August when WFMY in Greensboro went on the air. I saw my first television shows at a neighbor's house and wanted us to get a television right away, but my father waited for several months because he thought they were too expensive.

But soon trucks began stopping at houses on our block delivering television sets to our neighbors, and finally, in 1952, he decided to get one. He shopped around and finally bought an RCA Victor television from Milton McDade, a local Mebane merchant he had known for years. It was a heavy console, delivered by McDade and one of his helpers. Milton placed it in the corner of the living room, hooked it up to an antenna on top of the house, and explained the basic directions for operating the set. He also had lunch with us.

Finally, more than three years after this wondrous invention had come to Mebane, we were getting a television. After waiting so long to buy one, my parents now allowed it to become the center of the living room.

Getting a television presented a new moral issue for our home. My parents had always been against going to the movies on Sunday, but now television had invaded our home, and that seemed to raise the moral issue since it was really just a convenient and miniaturized version of the movies. They resolved the dilemma easily. Television, they reasoned, was really just radio with pictures, and we had always listened to radio on Sunday. Besides, we weren't really paying to watch television on Sundays like we would have to if we went to the movies. Additionally, several good programs aired on Sunday, like *The Ed Sullivan Show*. Problem solved.

In those early days of television, both channels carried programs from CBS, NBC, ABC, and Dumont. The picture was black and white, you had to get up and walk across the room to change the channel or adjust the picture or volume, and the channel went off at midnight with the playing of "The Star Spangled Banner" and did not return until seven o'clock the next morning. Still, it seemed like a wonderful invention, bringing comedies, dramas, ballgames, soap operas, game shows, local and national news, and so much more right into our living room.

We rarely missed *The Jackie Gleason Show*, *Your Show of Shows* (with Sid Caesar and Imogene Coco), *Arthur Godfrey and His Friends*, and the evening local and national news. One of our favorite television shows was *Your Hit Parade*, which debuted on NBC in 1950 after fifteen years as a popular radio program. The Hit Parade Orchestra and singers (the Lucky Strike Gang, named after the show's sponsor) performed the top seven songs of the week, with the number-one song always the last number, along with a couple other songs called "extras." At the end of show, Snooky Lanson, Dorothy Collins, Russell Arms, Giselle Mackenzie, and others would sing, "So long for awhile...that's all the songs for awhile."

But then rock-and-roll music hit in the mid-1950s, and the Lucky Strike Gang just couldn't do justice to "Rock Around the Clock," "Hound Dog," or the other teenage hits of the decade. I quickly lost interest, for I wanted to hear the rock songs performed by the original performers, not by these throwbacks to an earlier era. *Your Hit Parade* faded in the second half of the decade and went off the air in 1959, the year I graduated from high school. I preferred *American Bandstand*, which began on a Philadelphia television station in the early 1950s and then on ABC in 1957. It was getting more and more difficult for family members to enjoy the same music.

The annual Miss America Pageant hosted by the ever-smiling Bert Parks always drew a large television audience. The pageant was first televised in 1954, and after Parks debuted as the host of the show, he helped propel

Miss North Carolina Beauty Pageant contestants ride the Kiwanis Train at Burlington City Park in 1954. *Courtesy of Don Bolden.*

it to the top of the ratings the following year. Fans could barely contain their excitement when the winner was chosen from the finalists and Parks serenaded her with, "There she is, Miss America." Sponsored by the Junior Chamber of Commerce (Jaycees), the Miss North Carolina pageant was held in Burlington at Williams High School, which had the only auditorium in the county large enough to accommodate this hugely popular event, in 1951, 1954, and 1957. Beauty contests and parades were held in several Alamance County towns and attracted large crowds, particularly on Main Street in Burlington.

In 1963, Miss Jeanne Swanner of Graham won the Miss North Carolina title and the "Miss Congeniality" title. At six-foot-two, she was the tallest contestant in the Miss America Pageant, where she was also chosen as "Miss Congeniality." Most of her wardrobe was tailored from corduroy made in Haw River. Afterward, she embarked on a successful national career as a standup comedienne, toastmaster, and motivational speaker.

The new member of our household quickly changed many of our basic living habits. We stopped listening to our favorite radio shows, and indeed many of them (like Jack Benny and others) were beginning to go off the air and into oblivion if they couldn't make the transition to the new medium.

We timed our bathroom trips to commercial breaks. We sat on the porch less and eventually got an air conditioner so we could be comfortable inside the house as we watched our favorite programs. We sat in semidarkness, with the room lit by a small television light on a flower holder on top of the television. Subtly, advertising affected what we bought at the stores and convinced us that TV dinners were not only convenient but tasty as well. Sadly, neighbors and relatives visited less often, tied as they were to the schedules of their own favorite television shows.

Television brought entertainment and information into our house from all across the world. It gradually began to fill up our time, stealing hours away from porch-sitting, reading, conversation, dinner, and many other activities. But once it came into our house, it was there to stay.

Chapter 6
FOR EVERYTHING THERE WAS A SEASON

One of best things about living in Mebane and Alamance County was their location near the center of the state, between the mountains and the coast. This put us within easy driving distance of both and made it possible for us to enjoy the natural progression of the four seasons, each with its own beauty, characteristics, challenges, and opportunities.

Summer

My favorite season was summer. For a child like me, its arrival meant that the living would be easy, one fun-filled day after another. No school, no homework. It was time to play, read, sleep late, and do pretty much what I wanted to.

Although Alamance County was in the upper South, it still got hot in the summer, and we dealt with it the way most southerners did in this era before the widespread use of air conditioners. It was just part of living in the South; we expected it, and we learned to live with it.

Our small house had high ceilings and big window fans. We wore loose-fitting cotton clothing. We drank plenty of ice water, soft drinks, homemade lemonade, or sweet iced tea and sometimes tried to stir up a breeze with hand-held funeral home fans. On weekends, we gathered with relatives and sometimes neighbors in our backyard under a huge oak tree to cut an ice-cold watermelon or make homemade ice cream in a hand-turned ice cream churn. If possible, we did the hardest work in the early morning and late afternoon. If we were traveling long distances by car, like to the beach, we tried to travel at night or began the trip long before daylight in order to take advantage of the cooler temperatures.

After supper, we tried to cool off by sitting on our front porch on the shady side of the house, and at night, we slept with the windows open to let in the cool evening air. It also let in the sounds of summer—crickets chirping, dogs barking, people walking by and talking, neighbors shouting and arguing or playing their radios or televisions too loud, cars going by and, at regular intervals, the mournful whistle of a train slowly passing through our sleepy little town. Sometimes it was so hot that we had trouble sleeping, tossing and turning as we sweated into the sheets. We used small and large rotating fans, but they often just seemed to circulate the warm moist air instead of actually cooling us off.

My boyhood, from its early days on, was a happy one—the innocent, sheltered, uncomplicated boyhood possible in a small town in the late 1940s and 1950s. It was a good time to be a kid. I did have a few chores to do around the house as I got older. I carried buckets of coal into the house from the shed and lugged five-gallon cans of kerosene from Freshwater's Grocery. I also mowed the yard, raked leaves, worked in the garden, took out the garbage, brought in dry clothes off the clothesline, and sometimes rushed out to gather them when we heard the rumble of an approaching thunderstorm. Although I sometimes griped about my chores, they really weren't burdensome at all.

Summertime was a good time to explore the neighborhood and the town. Mebane was a safe town, and from a young age, I was allowed to roam in our neighborhood, adjacent neighborhoods and, eventually, all across town, traveling by foot or bicycle. There were so many young boys in the neighborhood that there was never a problem getting companions for a bike ride, cowboys and Indians, or a ballgame of some kind.

Most of the neighborhood kids I ran with were from middle-class and lower middle-class homes, the children of factory workers or downtown merchants who had lived in Mebane or outlying rural areas for most, if not all, of their lives. Most of the parents had not finished high school, much less college. Most of us came from traditional two-parent families, but there were exceptions.

A photograph of my niece Brenda Kelly's birthday party (she was three) in September 1950 captured much of the neighborhood gang. Taken by

Carr Street neighborhood children enjoy a birthday party for three-year-old Brenda Kelly (center), niece of the author (the tall guy on the back row), in the mid-1950s. *Courtesy of Velma Kelly.*

local professional photographer William Lynch, the photograph appeared in the *Mebane Enterprise* that month. The accompanying caption noted that "assisting Mrs. Oakley and Mrs. Kelly with the entertainment were Mrs. Herbert Payne and Mrs. Wyatt Phelps. Games were played, followed by the cutting of the traditional birthday cake, served with ice cream, cookies and candy."

Our parents encouraged us to go outside and play, and we did. We kept order among ourselves, without much adult supervision. We were never bored. There was never enough time to do everything we wanted to do during those long, delicious, hot summers when the world, or at least the neighborhood, seemed to belong to us. When we were very young, we entertained ourselves with metal or rubber toy trucks and cars in our backyard sand piles and played cowboys and Indians, riding our stick horses and shooting at one another with toy cap pistols and rifles. I kept these weapons by my bed at night like I knew any good cowboy would have done.

Sometimes we played war games, with the Americans always beating the Germans and Japanese like we saw in the Mebane Theater in movies made about World War II. We rode our Radio Flyer tricycles, wagons, scooters,

The author enjoying a day in the front yard of his home in the mid-1940s. *Courtesy of the author.*

and pedal cars, and as we got older and graduated to bicycles, we were able to range farther and farther from home.

We played red light, hide-and-seek, red rover, hopscotch, all kinds of ball, horseshoes, croquet, marbles, and cops and robbers. We flew kites and balsa wood gliders and caught June bugs, tied thread to their legs, and then flew them like kites. At dusk, we caught fireflies and put them in jars with holes punched in the metal lids to let in air so they wouldn't die.

We went blackberry picking, often coming back with as many chiggers and ticks as berries. We ate the blackberries by themselves, in a pie, or in a bowl with milk. No matter how we ate them, they were always a special treat.

If the weather was too hot to play strenuous games, we sat on pallets under a shade tree or on a porch and enjoyed a game of Rook, Monopoly, checkers, dominoes, Chinese checkers, or Clue. We played with Duncan yo-yos, Fly-Back paddleballs, and Slinkies, introduced right after the war and selling for about a dollar. We also played electric (battery-powered) baseball and basketball board games—always a pleasant way to spend rainy afternoons when we couldn't get outside to play the real thing.

When Carr was still a dirt street, we played softball, baseball, and football in it (sometimes joined by adults), but as we got older, we played on empty lots in our neighborhood and across town and eventually on the playground and basketball court constructed at E.M. Yoder School about a block from my house. Sometimes we went swimming at Back Creek, Cook's Mill, or Forest Lake. When I got into my teens, we traveled by bus or with older friends who could drive to Burlington to swim at the YMCA or at Lloyd's, a privately run swimming pool.

Some of my friends joined one of the Boy Scout troops at local churches. Soon they were reading the scout manual, *Handbook for Boys*, as if it were the

Bible. I went to a couple of scout meetings and camped out one night with another scout just to see if I liked it. I didn't. I didn't enjoy sleeping on the hard ground in the woods away from modern conveniences, and I didn't want to undergo the training and hardships necessary to get merit badges or progress to Eagle Scout rank. My interests lay elsewhere. I preferred the baseball field and basketball court to the woods, and *Sport Magazine* and the *Sporting News* to scouting publications.

Many factories and businesses in Alamance County closed for vacation during the Fourth of July week, but since we didn't have a car, we rarely took a summer vacation. Those who did typically went to the beach, usually to Carolina Beach near Wilmington, which had become a popular resort back in the 1880s. In the early 1950s, it was crowded in the summer with people from all across North Carolina and neighboring states seeking its beaches, amusement rides, shops, boardwalk, and cottages and small hotels. It was a blue-collar beach, drawing factory workers and other working-class people and servicemen from eastern North Carolina's military bases. Carolina Beach was devastated in 1954 by Hurricane Hazel, and after that, beachgoers headed farther south to the Myrtle Beach area instead. Carolina Beach never fully recovered, and Myrtle Beach has never stopped growing.

The author poses with his nieces Diana Payne, Brenda Kelly, and Kay Payne at Carolina Beach in the mid-1950s. *Courtesy of the author.*

My first trips to the beach were day trips. I was about twelve years old when my sister Colleen and my brother-in-law Herbert took my parents and me to Carolina Beach, where I saw the ocean for the first time. Leaving early in the morning, we traveled narrow, two-lane highways some two hundred miles to the coast in a car with no air conditioning, which few people had at the time. We changed into our bathing suits at a public bathhouse and spent the rest of the day on the beach. I swam in the ocean and looked at the young girls in bathing suits.

We left for home around suppertime, and the drive back was agonizing because it was so hot in the car and we had all gotten badly sunburned. But it had been worth it.

Fall

All too soon, August came, and with it the realization that summer vacation was drawing to a close and the end of our freedom was near. Although summer didn't officially come to a close until September 21, it ended for us on the day in early September when we trudged back to school with our new clothes, notebooks and pencils, and the anticipation of having new teachers, seeing old friends, and making new ones.

Summer was a special time for me growing up, but so was fall, with its shortening but still warm days, the golden hue cast by the setting sun, the full harvest moon, and the smell of burning leaves that had been raked to the ditch. We put our baseball gloves away, but they were still within handy reach in case we had a few days of unseasonably warm weather. We played basketball on outdoor courts with the backboard and goal nailed to a tree, and we had touch football games on the field of E.M. Yoder School lasting until dark on school days and from after lunch until dark on Saturdays and Sundays, no matter how cold or rainy it was.

Fall also brought the county fair to Mebane, as it had for decades. I always looked forward to riding the Ferris wheel; throwing balls at bottles or playing other games that took my money and, at best, gave back a small prize; and eating candied apples, popcorn, and hot dogs. I was always lured, too, to the front of the tent where the Hoochie-Coochie show was held. A scantily clad woman danced on a stage outside while the barker tried to lure the men standing around to "come on inside and see more than you've ever seen before." Afraid that someone might tell my parents, I never went in, but I noticed that several men I knew did, furtively looking around to see if anyone they knew might spot them going in to the sexually charged belly dance.

Fall also brought Friday night high school football games on the rocky field just down the street from the school. The field was also the site of the Fall Festival, run by the school and townspeople as a fundraiser for the school.

If the weather was simply too cold or rainy to play football on Sunday, I watched the Washington Redskins play on television. Although baseball still reigned as the national pastime at the professional and amateur level, professional football was making great gains in the 1950s as television exposed more people to the game. For years, one of the few professional games available on television in our area was the Washington Redskins' Sunday afternoon game. There were no professional football teams in the South, so from Washington to Miami, the Redskins were the favorite team of most southerners.

The Redskins had a fanatical following in the South, thanks to their proximity to the region, the promotional efforts of owner George Preston Marshall, and the growing popularity of television. Marshall systematically courted the South as his fan base. He recruited players from southern colleges, like Charlie "Choo-Choo" Justice from the University of North Carolina; scheduled several preseason games in southern cities like Columbia, Raleigh, and Winston-Salem; was a tireless speaker at civic clubs in the South; and booked southern high school bands to come to Washington to play at halftime. He recruited no black players until he signed Bobby Mitchell in 1962, becoming one of the last pro football team owners to integrate his team.

Marshall was quick to see the advantages of the new television medium. Beginning in 1950, just one year after Channel 2 came on the air in Greensboro, the Amoco Network telecast Redskins games all over the Southeast, building a large and fanatical regional audience for the games.

Marshall's techniques worked. With a mediocre team that had fallen from its former greatness, he filled the stadium with screaming fans at every home game while millions were glued to their black-and-white television sets. Spectators at the stadium and in front of their television sets at home couldn't get enough of the game and the halftime shows, which featured marching bands playing "Hail to the Redskins" with lines like "Fight for Old Dixie" and "Scalp 'em and swamp 'em, we'll take um big score."

On Halloween, downtown Mebane would be crowded with young and old taking on new identities as ghosts, goblins, witches, and other creatures associated with this medieval holiday. From there, the younger ones went out into the residential areas to trick-or-treat with no fear of being kidnapped or given candy laced with poison or razor blades.

A few weeks later, our family gathered around a bountiful meal to celebrate Thanksgiving, which we regarded as the real beginning of winter. Sometimes the males gathered in front of the black-and-white television for the annual Thanksgiving Day game between the Green Bay Packers and Detroit Lions.

Winter

Winters in Alamance County were not usually harsh, but we did have occasional snows, including twenty-four inches in 1940 and snowfalls on three consecutive Wednesdays in March 1960 that totaled close to eighteen inches. We rarely had enough accumulation to make snowmen, but sometimes we were lucky and did get enough snow or ice to go sledding on the road beside our house and anywhere we could find a hill; we used sleds, cafeteria trays, straight-backed wooden chairs, and anything else that would slide.

Carr Street neighbor Jerry West poses in the snow at the Oakley house. *Courtesy of the author.*

A large crowd waiting for the first glimpse of Santa in downtown Graham, 1961. *Courtesy of the Graham Historical Museum.*

When I was child, Christmas was a special time, not just the long shopping period between Thanksgiving and the end of the business day on December 24. A few days after Thanksgiving, I would pore over our Sears & Roebuck Christmas catalog and send my wish list in a letter to Santa Claus at the North Pole. Christmas parades were held in Mebane, Burlington, and Graham. We always went to the Mebane Christmas parade, to the Christmas pageant held in the fellowship hall of the Methodist Church, and to the Christmas parties at school. We decorated a big cedar tree in the living room and bought a country ham and other Christmas goodies at Freshwater's Grocery, and for several days before Christmas, Mother and Aunt Mae filled our house with the wonderful aroma of cakes, pies, cookies, and other favorites they were cooking up for the holidays.

My father used his Christmas savings at the bank and his Christmas bonus from Kingsdown to pay off some of his bills and buy Christmas gifts. A few days before Christmas, we usually rode the bus or train to Burlington for a full day of shopping and a hot dog meal at Zack's.

At a time when children received few toys during the year, few things in life could match the excitement of the night before Christmas and the following morning. After a virtually sleepless night, I got up and opened my gifts and then made the rounds of the neighborhood to see what Santa Claus had brought my friends. No matter how cold it was, we usually headed to the ball field to try out our new baseball gloves and other sports equipment.

Sometimes we got an early winter treat with a surprise snow around Christmas that magically transformed our working-class neighborhood into a winter wonderland. Snow meant snow cream, snowball fights, snowmen, and sledding. Most of all, it meant no school, sometimes for several days. It didn't snow often, but it was always a treat when it did.

Spring

Winter became inconvenient and tiresome after awhile, but spring always arrived, bringing a gradual thaw from the cold winter along with violent thunderstorms, Easter, Mother's Day, and May Day and other end-of-the-year activities at school. It also brought the start of the baseball season and dreams (hopeless ones, it turned out) of becoming a major-league baseball star. But best of all, spring brought the promise that school would soon let out for the summer, when we would start the cycle of the seasons all over again.

Chapter 7
BASEBALL

A large part of my boyhood was taken up with sports—football, basketball, tennis, horseshoes, tetherball, croquet, roller bat, and baseball. But it was baseball that I loved the most.

I wasn't alone. Although football and basketball and other sports grew rapidly in the postwar period, baseball was still the national pastime, still the most popular participant and spectator sport. Most Americans, male and female, had played it or its close kin softball growing up, and its games were eagerly followed from the major leagues on down through the minor leagues, industrial and church leagues, semipro leagues, high schools and colleges, and even pickup sandlot games. It was a common bond for millions of Americans.

Some of my earliest memories of playing are of playing roller bat, softball, and baseball with other neighborhood kids. We played wherever and whenever we could, even in the winter, when it was so cold that catching or hitting the ball stung our hands. There were a lot of children in our neighborhood, so it usually wasn't difficult to get a game together.

Baseball gave us young males a common bond. All season long, we played it and talked about it with one another and with adults who shared our passion, and we discussed it during the off-season as well. We all had our favorite ballplayers and major-league teams—it was something you had to have as part of the group. My favorite players were Jackie Robinson, Pee Wee Reese, Duke Snider, and the rest of the Brooklyn Dodgers, even though every year I saw these idols go down to defeat in

Cover of an early 1950s comic book about Jackie Robinson. *Courtesy of the Library of Congress.*

Opposite: Cover of *Sport Magazine* featuring slugger Mickey Mantle. *Courtesy of the author.*

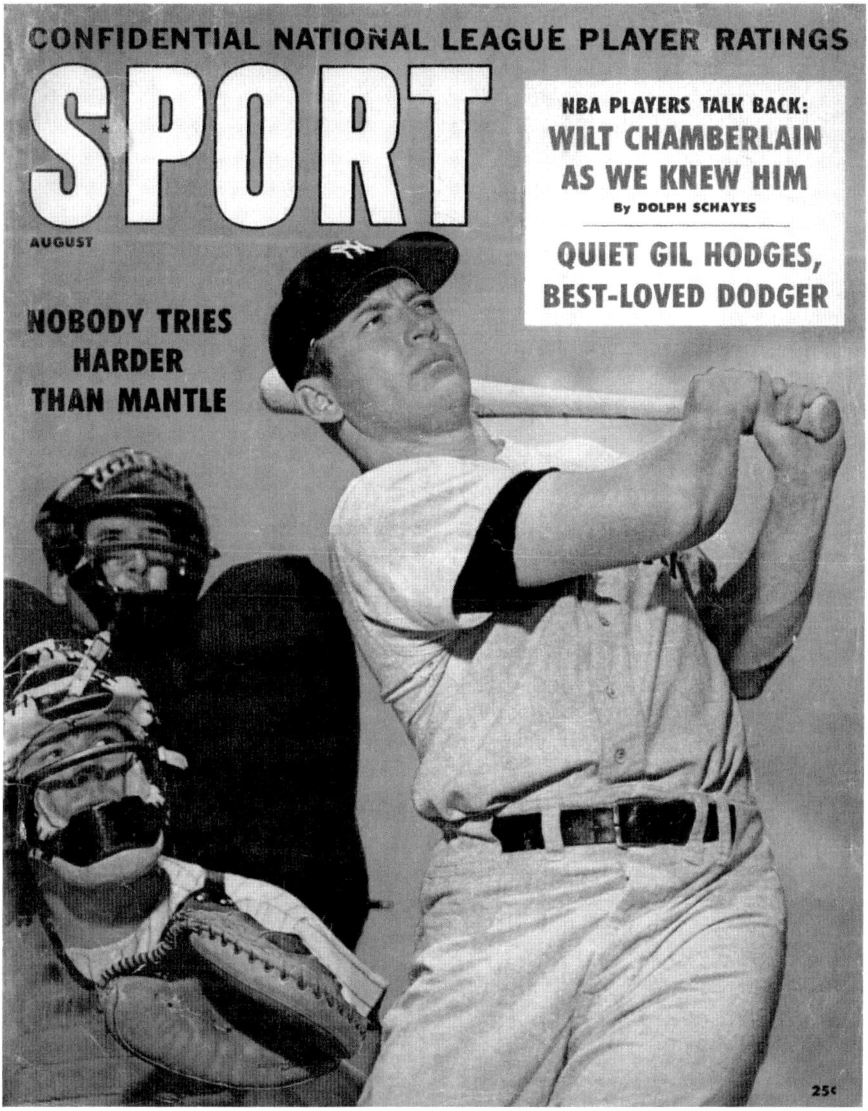

the World Series against Mickey Mantle, Yogi Berra, and the rest of the New York Yankees.

We kept up with the game on the radio, in newspapers and magazines, and, eventually, on television. We followed the pennant races from the first pitch in the spring to the last out in the World Series in October, when we listened to the games over the intercom system at school after lunch and then hurried home after school to catch the end of it on the radio or television.

(There were no night World Series games then.) We memorized endless reams of statistics about teams, players, pennant races, and great games. We traded baseball cards, magazines, and comic books and talked about the games frequently, even during the "hot stove league" in the fall and winter, when football and basketball were temporarily allowed into the spotlight.

Television opened up a whole new window to baseball for me. Before television came to our house, I followed the national pastime through the newspapers, the *Sporting News* and other magazines, radio, and the brief clips on the news at the movie theaters on Saturday afternoon. Now with television, I could see my favorite teams and players perform on "The Game of the Week" with Dizzy Dean, Buddy Blattner, and, later, Pee Wee Reese. The screen was small, but it brought the game into our house like it had never been before.

I was sure I wanted to be a major-league ballplayer when I grew up, a fantasy shared by millions of other young boys in the late 1940s and the 1950s. I talked about it, dreamed about it, and prayed that it would happen.

When I got older, I played in the summertime in a program sponsored by the Mebane Recreation Department. We practiced two afternoons a week and played games with teams from Altamahaw-Ossippee, Saxapahaw, Swepsonville, Haw River, and other nearby mill towns. I was usually stationed at third base or the outfield. We played on hard, rocky infields and outfields checkered with a little scrub grass and bounded by aging wooden fences, and the games were umpired by local men who had trouble disguising their affections for the home team. At the Swepsonville field, a river rather than a fence marked the end of the outfield. Any ball hit into the river was an automatic home run.

One of the best things about playing for the recreation department was that once a week we took the activity bus to Burlington Park to go swimming at the YMCA. It was so much better than swimming in the lakes and creeks I swam in growing up.

We were great fans of the game at all levels, especially the major leagues. The major-league game we loved was far away, and most of us knew we might never have a chance to watch a major-league game in person—the sixteen teams were concentrated in ten cities in the Northeast and Midwest. Alamance County had sent several native sons to the major leagues, including Graham's Tom Zachary and Mebane's Lew Riggs.

Zachary was a star pitcher for the Washington Senators and several other teams, but he is best remembered as the man who threw Babe Ruth the pitch that Ruth hit out of the park for his record sixtieth home run in 1927.

Mebane native and major leaguer Lew Riggs reaches for the ball. *Courtesy of Mebane Historical Museum.*

Riggs played third base for the Cardinals, Cincinnati Reds, and Brooklyn Dodgers; participated in the 1936 All-Star Game and the 1940 and 1941 World Series; and then missed the next three seasons while he served in World War II. Like many players of that era, he returned from those lost years with age and the layoff having eroded his skills. He played only one more major-league game, in 1946 with the Dodgers, giving him a total of 760 major league-games with twenty-eight home runs and a lifetime batting average of .262. He spent the years 1946–50 playing for Montreal, St. Paul, Newark, and Baltimore, never again getting the call to the majors. In 1951, he returned to his hometown and opened a shoe store on Clay Street with his brother, Hurley.

I delivered newspapers to Lew's home and went by his store every Saturday to collect forty cents and to talk about baseball and other sports. He loved to reminisce about baseball but was always modest about his own achievements. He often talked about the players he knew, his most memorable games, the joy of playing, and the boredom of frequent train travel and hotel changes. When I asked him about Jackie Robinson, who played with him at Montreal, he always praised Robinson's talent and courage and frequently called him "one heck of a ballplayer."

Minor League Baseball

The only professional baseball teams most of us ever saw growing up were the minor-league teams. Minor-league baseball boomed after the war, just like the majors, with teams and leagues sprouting up in big and small towns all across the country. North Carolina was one of the nation's leading states in the number of minor-league teams and leagues. In the late 1940s, there were eight leagues and forty-nine teams in the state.

The league in our area was the Class B Carolina League, founded in 1944. Its attendance boomed to over 1 million in 1947 but then quickly fell as television and other forms of entertainment took away many of the fans and dollars. By 1952, attendance barely reached 500,000. Still, while some other minor leagues in the state and nation died in the 1950s, the Carolina League survived. Its fans followed their teams (Greensboro, Reidsville, Danville, Durham, Raleigh, Winston-Salem, Fayetteville, and Burlington) by going out to the local park, carpooling to attend games with rivals in nearby cities, listening to them on the radio, and reading accounts of their games in the local newspapers, which gave their local teams almost as much space as those in the majors.

For us, live professional baseball meant going to Burlington or Durham to see the Class B minor-league teams. Most of the games were at night, following the growing practice all across the nation in minor- and major-league parks as clubs tried to make the game more accessible to working people who couldn't attend in the daytime.

Near the end of May 1952, the *Burlington Daily-Times News* began to carry the rumor that Ron Necciai would soon be pitching for the Bur-Gra Pirates. We had already heard about the nineteen-year-old string bean (six-foot-three and 165 pounds) pitcher with the blazing fastball that had earned him the nicknames "Rocket Ron" and the "Bristol Pistol." Early in the spring, playing in the Class D Appalachian League in the little mountain town of Bristol on the Virginia-Tennessee border, he struck out twenty in his first game, nineteen in his second, a record eleven in a row in relief, and then a record twenty-seven in a no-hitter. News of this feat was broadcast in hundreds of newspaper and magazine articles, and reporters and Major League Baseball officials began calling him the next Dizzy Dean or Bob Feller.

Bur-Gra Pirates strikeout pitcher "Rocket Ron" Necciai in 1952. *Courtesy of Don Bolden.*

Not long after he arrived in Burlington, I finally got to see him pitch. I stood along the fence behind the dugout with several other fans, old and young, hoping he would come over and sign our programs. He did, along with several other Burlington players. I don't remember how well he pitched that night, but at the time, it was enough just to see him up close and get his autograph.

I saw him pitch on two other occasions, but as the summer

progressed and the Pirates remained in the cellar, his newspaper coverage gradually decreased. On August 2, he pitched his last game for the local Pirates, beating the Raleigh Caps 5–0 and striking out seventeen. For close to two months, he had provided a welcome diversion from the hapless play of the Bur-Gra Pirates, who finished dead last in the league with a 45-92 record, 34½ games behind the Raleigh Caps.

Necciai's jump from Class D ball at Bristol to the parent club in less than three months was too ambitious. Suffering from control problems, a sore arm, and stomach and other illnesses, he could muster only a 1-7 record with thirty-one strikeouts and a 7.08 ERA in 54.2 innings. It was his first, and last, major-league season.

Semipro baseball and softball also thrived after World War II. Most of the semipro players worked at another job during the day and played ball at night. Some factories even recruited players to play for their teams, finding jobs for them or giving them easy jobs that would enable them to save their strength for the night game that might bring reflected glory on the factory if the team won. Like minor-league ball, semipro ball was hurt by television and other contenders for the entertainment dollar and time. As the 1950s wore on, men who might have played ball after work spent their time with their families or on the golf course or the lake.

In 1958, the Dodgers and Giants played in their new homes on the West Coast. It was the end of my junior year. It was harder to be a Dodgers fan—their home games were played three hours later and often didn't make the morning papers. Plus, Jackie Robinson and some of my other favorites had retired.

Not long after I entered high school, my passion for baseball began to cool. I moved on to other interests—my job at the drugstore, the high school basketball team, tennis, books and reading, and girls. I still followed the game in the newspapers and occasionally on television, but I gave my bat, glove, and baseball cards and magazines and books to my nephew. I had long ago given up my unrealistic boyhood dream of becoming a major-league baseball player and began to think about making a living as a pharmacist or a teacher or writer—all far cries from the glamour of the major-league diamond.

Chapter 8

THE BIGGEST LITTLE TOWN ON EARTH

In the 1950s, Mebane entered the second half of the twentieth century as a stable and prosperous little town. It seemed frozen in time, like the American communities depicted in the nostalgic Norman Rockwell covers on the *Saturday Evening Post.*

Concentrated for a mile along several blocks paralleling the Southern Railway tracks and Highway 70, Mebane was still a railroad town in the 1950s, just as it had been since its founding back in the middle of the nineteenth century. Several passenger and freight trains passed through town every day and throughout the night, sometimes blocking traffic as they passed or when they stopped to route freight cars onto sidetracks serving downtown industries.

Inevitably, frustrated motorists tried to cross the tracks before the train arrived, and inevitably there were unlucky ones who lost that race and were hit by a speeding locomotive. Several people were killed over the years, including four members of one family who died in a horrible train-car crash just outside of town.

Mebane was often described by locals as the "biggest little town on earth." In the compact downtown area, which was within walking distance of several neighborhoods, residents had easy access to medical offices, the post office, several clothing and shoe stores, grocery stores, restaurants, drugstores, auto dealerships, service stations, barbershops, flower shops, a photography studio, pool halls, the bus and train stations, the public library, and the Mebane Theater. Mebane also had a garden club, book club, music club, two civic clubs (Kiwanis and Exchange Club), and a nine-hole golf course.

There were several full-service gas stations in town. Most people called them filling stations. While you sat in the car, the attendant filled your tank with gasoline (costing about twenty-five cents a gallon), checked your oil and antifreeze, and cleaned the windshield. Stations also fixed flat tires and made minor repairs.

Most people worked in local retail stores, textile mills, Craftique Furniture Company, White Furniture Company, or the Kingsdown mattress and bedding company. Several hundred others drove to nearby Burlington to work in hosiery mills or the booming Western Electric Company.

The biggest employer in town was White Furniture Company. For decades, townspeople told time by its whistle, which blew during the workweek to signal its employees and many townspeople when to come to work, take a break, have lunch, return to work, take another break, and, finally, go home for the day.

In this friendly town of a little over 2,200 people, everyone seemed to know one another. If you walked down the streets, you knew most of the merchants inside the stores and almost everyone you passed on the street. Merchants readily cashed your checks or extended credit because they knew you and your family. Credit cards, of course, were virtually unheard of.

Mebane was a walkers' town. Small and compact, it was easy for most people who lived in the city limits to walk to town and all over the town's central business district to shop or pay bills. Traffic was light, and much of the time there seemed to be little need for the seven stoplights. Year round, hot or cold, rainy or dry, many people walked to work, to school, to the grocery store, to the medical clinic, and to the dentist. If you bought something too heavy to carry, you could get it delivered. If you needed your television repaired, Milton McDade came to your house. Around town, you might see someone riding a bike or walking for exercise, but you rarely saw a jogger. If you saw someone running, you assumed that he was trying to get somewhere fast or had done something he shouldn't have.

Factory workers lived in generally well-kept frame mill houses or former mill houses near the factories where they worked or in the new housing developments springing up just outside the city limits. There were distinct class divisions. Many residents—prosperous merchants, doctors, dentists, and the owners or top managers of the businesses and industries—lived on South Fifth Street or in the new Forest Lake development on the north edge of town. South Fifth Street was a mixture of well-kept older homes adorned in the spring with beautiful dogwoods and azaleas. Forest Lake was much more secluded, with most of the homes nestled in the woods by the lake.

Mebane was a safe town. Children played in their yards and neighborhoods and rode bicycles all over town without their parents fearing that they might be kidnapped or harmed in some other way. People left their houses unlocked during the day and often at night, spoke to one another and to strangers on the street, were not afraid to let door-to-door salesmen in their homes, and left their keys in the car when it was parked in the driveway and sometimes even in front of downtown stores or in the parking lot of their workplaces. Robberies and vandalism were rare, drugs were what you bought at the drugstore to cure an ailment of some kind, and murders, rapes, riots, and other human-caused calamities were things that happened somewhere else, mostly in big cities. In this peaceful little town, a three-man police department led by Chief Buck Smith seemed an almost unnecessary precaution.

Bible Belt

Mebane was part of the Bible Belt. There was strong social pressure to belong to a church and to attend regularly. Everybody in town knew whether you went to church or not and to which church you belonged. One of the first questions asked of visitors or newcomers was, "What church do you go to?"

Many Protestant denominations were represented among the several churches scattered across town, but most white Mebane residents belonged to the big three located downtown—First United Methodist Church, the First Presbyterian Church, and the First Baptist Church—and to the fundamentalist churches scattered around town. The black population attended separate churches on the outskirts of town. The nearest Catholic church was the Blessed Sacrament Church in Burlington. On Sunday, downtown retail stores, grocery stores, the Mebane Theater, and gas stations were closed, and the drugstores did not open until after lunch.

Few people were concerned about church and state separation. Once or twice a year, evangelists from churches outside of town came to preach in one of the churches or in the high school auditorium. In the fall of 1957, popular evangelist Leighton Ford led a weeklong "Mebane Evangelistic Crusade" held not just in the churches but also in the high school auditorium.

Mailmen Bill Warren and Paul Williams try a different way of delivering the mail. *Courtesy of Mebane Historical Museum.*

Mail, Telephones, and Telegrams

Mebane was a place where you could address a letter to "Mr. Jesse Oakley, Mebane" or simply "Mr. Jess Oakley, City" and it would be delivered to the correct mailbox. For many years, Mebane mail carriers walked their routes lugging their heavy bags. At times, they experimented with making their rounds on bicycles.

In the 1940s, telephone numbers had just four digits (ours was 4364), and for several years, we were on a party line with several talkative and sometimes nosy neighbors who listened to our conversations. Calls to Burlington, only ten miles away, were long distance and had to be dialed by an operator. Western Union telegrams could be sent from Carolina Drug Store.

Segregation

Mebane had the usual faults of small southern towns. It was a segregated community, with separate schools and other public facilities for blacks and whites. In the waiting room at the Mebane Clinic, blacks sat on one side and whites on the other, and at Alamance General Hospital in Burlington, white and black patients were housed in separate wards. Few patients, white or black, had health insurance. People paid what and when they could. Many farmers paid up once a year when they sold their tobacco crop.

Poverty and custom dictated that most black families lived in substandard housing in developments just off of Fifth Street in an area called West End, which paralleled the railroad track and Highway 70, or on tobacco farms out along Highway 119 North. All the churches were segregated, and there was only one black school, West End, an elementary school first built in 1937 and added on to in 1951 and 1958. Black students were bussed to Graham to go to high school. Whites and blacks also had separate funeral homes and cemeteries.

North of Mebane on Highway 119 was a historical area in the Cross Roads community where many whites and blacks shared a common history and biological lineage going back to the days of slavery, worshipping together in Cross Roads Presbyterian Church and being buried in its cemetery in the white section or the slave section. As a young teenager, I sometimes rode by the church on my bicycle, but I didn't know of that rich heritage and wouldn't know until the 1977 television mini-series *Roots: The Saga of an American Family*, based on Alex Haley's book, captured the nation's attention. Haley visited the area while researching his book and returned in 1977 for a reunion at the church.

Growing up, I had no black neighbors, black schoolmates, black opponents on the sports teams we played against in high school sports, and no black friends my age. Almost all the black people I knew were adults. They were the people who picked up the garbage in our neighborhood, shined shoes at the barbershops, served as janitors or cooks in Mebane School, worked with my father at Kingsdown, or labored as yard boys or domestics at white people's homes. Virtually the only black people who ever came into the neighborhood were the garbage men, a tall black man who delivered coal and ice, and domestics who came in to do yard work, clean house, or tend to children.

Like typical white southerners, we grew up rarely questioning the segregation that was so deeply entrenched in our society. We grew up prejudiced against blacks as a group but were fond of many black individuals, like Alice, the black barbers at Tom Holt's barbershop, and the black men with whom my father worked at Kingsdown.

Tom Holt's Barbershop

My first black friends were the three barbers at Tom's, one of the two black-operated barbershops in town. Neither served black patrons. It was, in many ways, a different world from the white-operated shop (City Barber Shop) on Center Street. Tom's had the same familiar smell of shave cream, hair tonic, and talcum powder, but it was a much smaller shop, with only three barber chairs and an old deacon's bench for customers waiting their turn in the chair. At the back of the shop was a shoeshine stand. An adolescent black male, whom I knew only by his nickname, "Slick," was the shoeshine boy.

The shop's owner, Tom Holt, a polite, soft-spoken little man, had the chair next to the window. He had stood in that same place cutting white people's hair for many years, and he looked ancient. At the chair beside him was Fred Walker, a younger, taller, and heavier man who reminded me of Jackie Robinson. At the chair next to the shoeshine stand was a large friendly man named Wes, who walked with a distinct limp. I never knew his last name.

These were the first middle-class black men I had ever known, and they didn't fit the black stereotypes I had learned as a child. They wore white shirts and ties and talked and acted like the white businessmen and professionals around town. They always treated me like an adult, not a child. As I walked in the door, they all greeted me warmly with the words, "Come in, Mr. Oakley. Have a seat, and we'll be with you shortly." They carried on a running conversation about sports, the weather, and other safe topics with their customers in the chairs and those sitting on the deacon's bench waiting their turn. If you didn't feel like talking, you could read the shop's copies of the *Saturday Evening Post*, *Life* magazine, or the new magazine that debuted in 1954, *Sports Illustrated*.

When I sat down in the chair, I got the royal treatment. "Take a little off the top for you today, Mr. Oakley? How've you been doing? Are you making good grades in school again this year? How's your mother and daddy? That Mr. Jess is a funny man. We like it when he stops by and sticks his head in the door and hollers at us." (He did that frequently, but he always went to the white shop for his haircut.) When they finished cutting my hair, shaving around my ears and applying a generous amount of talcum powder, they turned me around so I could look in the mirror. "Does it look all right, Mr. Oakley?" It almost always did.

They soon learned that I was a baseball fan and that we had a mutual favorite team, the Brooklyn Dodgers. It was no coincidence that they were Dodger fans, for Brooklyn led the rest of the major leagues in integrating professional baseball in 1947, and Jackie Robinson was a major hero to black Americans and to many white ones as well. We talked baseball all year long, even in the winter, but the conversation really livened up in the spring. The radio was usually turned to a baseball game, and I would hardly get through the door before Fred would say something like, "Mr. Oakley, what do you think about the Dodgers' chances this year?" "I think they'll win it all," I'd reply, repeating what I had read in the newspapers or the *Sporting News*. Fred, a diehard Dodger fan but a great admirer of the Giants' Willie Mays, often asked, "Do you think the Duke will hit more homers than Willie this year?"

It would go on like this all summer. When the pennant races heated up in late summer, we talked about whether the Dodgers and Yankees would go at each other again and whether the Dodgers would be able to finally beat them this year. They loved the game of baseball, and although the growing presence of black players in the major leagues was an enormous source of pride, it was always clear that their love of baseball went far beyond racial pride in the Dodgers.

Occasionally I would mention that it was a real shame that Robinson and other blacks had been kept out of major-league baseball for so long. They always agreed but quickly mentioned that the times just weren't right before Robinson and then went on to other subjects. It was clear that they really felt a little uncomfortable discussing that with me. After all, I was white, and for all they knew, I could have repeated any comments they made about racial injustice around town, and it would have damaged their business. When I went in their shop, they always played the role of the professional but humble black businessmen.

Years later, I would wonder what they said about me when I left the shop after initiating a discussion about race relations. I wondered, too, how they really felt about having to bow and scrape before their white customers in order to make a living.

As I got to know them better over the years, I would often stop by between haircuts and stick my head in the door to chat with them briefly about baseball. I considered them my friends at a time when I had no black friends my own age, and my friendship with them brought my first questioning of the racism and segregation with which I grew up.

Mebane had the usual faults of most small southern towns. It had few professional jobs outside teaching and not enough middle-class jobs. It had no radio station or bookstore. Paperbacks could be bought from revolving circular stands in the drugstores for twenty-five or thirty-five cents, but for anything beyond that, you had to go to Alamance Book and Stationary Store in Burlington or to bookstores in Chapel Hill and Durham. It was the same for phonograph records. Reliable Furniture Company carried a small selection of records, but the nearest record shop was in Burlington. The closest upscale restaurants and movie theaters carrying first-run movies were also in Burlington.

The town had no radio station or daily newspaper. It did have a weekly newspaper, the *Enterprise*, which dated back to 1919. It was a small-town weekly carrying mostly local news about marriages and deaths, the annual county fair and Tobacco Festival, civic club meetings, church circles, residents' vacation trips to the coast or mountains, and other personal items. The September 18, 1952 edition noted that "Jack Latta of Oak Ridge spent the weekend with his parents, Mr. and Mrs. John Latta" and that "Mr. and Mrs. Satterfield visited Rover McAdams in Alamance General Hospital Sunday evening." Some of the notices of wedding parties and other events actually used the phrase "and a good time was had by all." The paper was deliberately targeted to a town in which everybody knew everybody else. There was very little county, state, national, or international news, and nothing from the wire service. People wanting to read about the world outside Mebane subscribed to the morning *Greensboro Daily News*, the *Durham Morning Herald* or the afternoon *Burlington Daily Times-News*.

Mebane had its prejudices, gossip, and scandals. In this small, close-knit town, personal and family secrets were hard to keep, and people gossiped about their neighbors, ministers, teachers, divorcées, second marriages, and unwed mothers. You knew who the town drunks were, who the philanderers were, whose car was parked in front of the widow's house, whose beat-up pickup was in front of the beer joint, and which high school girls were generous with their favors and which ones weren't.

Scandals and tragedies were talked about long after they had lost their freshness. Before television brought in so much news of the outside world and numbed us to scandals and tragedies by parading so many of them before our eyes, local events lingered long in people's minds.

But race relations were generally good at a time when tensions were rising and even exploding in towns and cities across the South. It was a place where neighbors collected money for flowers when someone died and brought food to the grieving family, where a "viewing" of the corpse at Walker's Funeral Home would draw hundreds of mourners along with professional funeral goers, and where you knew who was sick and who was getting better.

When Tobacco Was King

Tobacco was a natural and accepted part of our lives growing up. Tobacco products were heavily advertised on radio and television and in magazines and newspapers, often featuring promotions by movie and sports stars and with testimonials from physicians. Our elders told us not to smoke, that it stunted our growth and that it cut our wind, yet they continued to smoke in front of us.

In 1957, Surgeon General Leroy Burney announced that a study commission composed of doctors had concluded that "excessive cigarette smoking is one of the causative factors of lung cancer." But the American people continued to light up. After all, doctors, movie stars, star athletes, and other celebrities appeared smoking in magazine, newspaper, and television ads, and Edward R. Murrow and other television newsmen smoked on screen.

Most adult males and many teenagers used tobacco in some form. Our fathers smoked or chewed or both, and most of our male teachers smoked—we could see the cigarette packs in their pockets and smell the smoke on their breath and clothes. When I was in the seventh grade, a field trip to the Raleigh-Durham-Chapel Hill area included a tour of one of Durham's cigarette factories, where free cigarettes were given to our male teacher and our bus driver.

Very few women smoked—that was still regarded in many circles as unfeminine—but many, like my mother, aunts, and female neighbors, dipped snuff. Mother kept an empty coffee can nearby for her and her visitors to spit in as they talked and dipped. Several boys in our high school smoked, but not very many girls, at least not in public.

In the late summer and fall, Mebane was invaded by tobacco farmers and tobacco buyers from the major tobacco companies. The scent of tobacco lay heavy in the air, and the streets were crowded with farmers and their families using their profits from the golden leaf to pay off the past year's debts and buy school clothing and other necessities for the children. The tobacco auctions were a boon to the local merchants. Every August and September, the *Mebane Enterprise* was full of articles welcoming tobacco farmers to Mebane and advertising their products. When farmers were paid for their tobacco, they went to Mebane's retail stores to buy clothing, home appliances, grocery staples, and other necessities and to pay for goods and services they had charged during the past year.

During the tobacco auctions, the warehouse owners and local merchants sponsored several forms of entertainment to draw people to the downtown area. There were rides for the children, food of all kinds, a Tobacco Festival Parade featuring marching bands and floats with beauty queens, country music performers like Little Jimmy Dickens and other Grand Ole' Opry stars who put on a show in one of the warehouses, and the crowning of a Tobacco Queen, chosen from some of Mebane's prettiest girls.

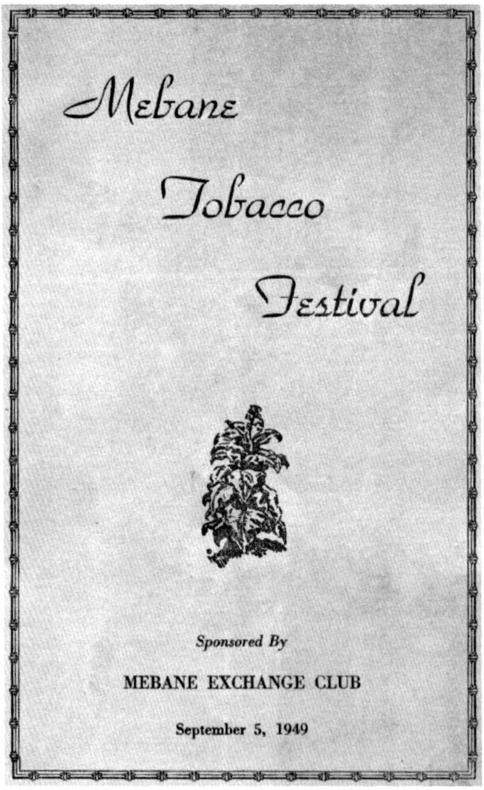

Tobacco Festival program cover. *Courtesy of Mebane Historical Museum.*

On weekends, the streets were roped off at some intersections for a street dance. When I was small, my sisters took me, and as I got older, I went by myself. The street dances seemed a little wicked—you could see people with beer bottles in their hands as they walked through the crowd or got out in a circle and showed off their dancing skills. The most spirited dancing occurred at the end of the main business district, on the corner of Clay and Second Streets, where black dancers showed off their moves. Whites and blacks did not dance with each other—that would have been asking for trouble.

Like so many other small towns, Mebane was distinctive in the 1950s, the era before the coming of the interstate

PROGRAM

1:00 P. M.	DOLLAR DUSTERS
2:00 P. M.	PARADE
3:00 P. M.	WATER POLO CONTEST
4:00 P. M.	MATINEE OF GRAND OLE OPRY
7:00 P. M.	GRAND OLE OPRY
9:00 P. M.	BEAUTY CONTEST
10:00 P. M.	TOBACCO BALL

HONOR GUESTS

W. KERR SCOTT, *Governor of North Carolina*
H. P. TAYLOR, *Lt.-Governor of North Carolina*
DAN K. EDWARDS, *Mayor of Durham, North Carolina*
R. C. GODWIN, *State Commander of American Legion*
JAMES MOORE, *Newspaper Publisher*

DOLLAR DUSTERS

At 1:00 P. M. an airplane will fly over the business district of the City of Mebane and from that plane 1000 redeemable checks valued at $1.00 each, will be dropped. Each of these checks will be redeemable at local stores named on the check.

Tobacco Festival schedule of events. *Courtesy of Mebane Historical Museum.*

system and other developments began eroding regional distinctions and homogenizing towns all across the nation. In this little town, it was easy to feel secure, isolated from problems people were facing in other parts of the nation and the world. Change seemed to come slowly, if at all, and it was easy to feel that Mebane would always remain the way it was when we were growing up.

But that was not to be.

Chapter 9

VISITING THE BIG CITY OF BURLINGTON

We didn't travel much when I was growing up. We had very little money, and our family didn't own an automobile. Most of our relatives lived in Carrboro and Burlington, and sometimes we'd catch a ride with a friend or neighbor to visit them. But unless they came to see us, the visits were few and far between.

One of the places we often went to was Burlington, by far the largest city in Alamance County and just ten miles west of Mebane on Highway 70. Sometimes we went by automobile or train, but usually we walked to town and caught the bus at Harry Dollar's bus station beside the Mebane Theater. With Highway 70 being a major thoroughfare in the center of the state, several buses came through Mebane every day, providing a comfortable and convenient ride to Durham or Raleigh in the east or Graham, Burlington, Greensboro, or High Point to the west. People who couldn't get to the bus station simply stood by the side of the road on Highway 70 and waited for the bus to stop and pick them up. Passengers wanting to get off between stops pulled an overhead cord that activated chimes to signal the bus driver, who then pulled over and stopped when it was safe to do so.

The bus went through Haw River and Graham, and we occasionally got off the bus in Graham to attend to government business, shop at W.S. Nick's General Merchandise Store, and enjoy a soft drink or ice cream treat at the Graham Soda Shop on Court Square. But usually we stayed on the bus until it rolled into downtown Burlington to the bus station on Maple Avenue.

Court Square in downtown Graham was a county government center and popular shopping destination. *Courtesy of Graham Historical Museum.*

Burlington was one of the major stations for Carolina Trailways, which inaugurated service in 1925 between Greensboro and Raleigh. From then on, bus travel increased dramatically. By the late 1940s, Burlington was the junction of bus routes running from Charlotte to Norfolk, New York to Florida, Norfolk to Memphis, and other points in all directions of the compass. In 1949, Carolina Trailways was operating 312 buses, and 76 buses left Burlington every day for cities across the state and the nation.

The bus and train stations were right downtown near the heart of the retail district, so it was easy to ride the bus or train to Burlington early in the morning, shop for most of the day, and return to Mebane before dinner.

Occasionally we traveled by train, buying our tickets at the Mebane train station and boarding the train with all the anticipation of someone taking a long trip. Passenger trains still stopped several times a day at the little Mebane train station, and we sometimes bought tickets to ride to Burlington or Greensboro for a day of shopping or just to take the train ride.

In the early 1950s, the railroads still carried far more passengers than the airlines, which were still shunned by many travelers as too expensive, too dangerous, and too novel. This changed as the decade wore on and more and more Americans were turning to private automobiles for short trips and airplanes for longer ones. Railroad ridership, which had stood at 916 million in 1944, dropped to 488 million passengers in 1950 and 327 million in 1960.

No matter how we got there, going to Burlington was always a special treat. For several years, it was the biggest town and had the tallest buildings I'd ever seen. One was the nine-story Atlantic Bank and Trust Company, built in 1929. It later became Security National Bank, NCNB, and, eventually, the LabCorp headquarters. Another imposing structure was the Alamance Hotel on the corner of Maple Avenue and South Main Street, which advertised in 1957 that its amenities included "all rooms with bath and circulating water."

Some of the Burlington retail stores were two stories tall and had elevators, which were absent from Mebane's small one-story establishments. They also had separate public restrooms and drinking fountains labeled "Whites Only" or "Colored."

Above: Downtown Burlington was still a thriving retail center in 1961. *Courtesy of Walter Boyd.*

Left: Downtown Burlington, 1963. *Courtesy of Walter Boyd.*

In the early 1950s, Burlington had a population of around twenty-five thousand (ten times that of Mebane), two radio stations, several restaurants, a public library, a business college, a small liberal arts college (Elon), a large city park, and a professional minor-league baseball team. Downtown Burlington had a Sears and a J.C. Penney store and upscale department stores like Belk-Beck, B.A. Sellers and Son, and Efird's. Most of these stores offered layaway plans, which allowed customers to put Christmas gifts on layaway at stores and pay so much each week or month until Christmas. The sidewalks were often crowded with shoppers, and sometimes on Saturday we saw a street preacher downtown walking back and forth with a Bible in his hand warning people to repent and accept Jesus as their savior or else go to hell.

One of my favorite stores was the Sears and Roebuck Store on Front Street. With two stories, it was one of the biggest stores I had ever seen and had a large selection of baseball equipment and toys. As I got older, I spent less time at Sears and more time browsing the books on the shelves of at the Alamance Book and Stationery Store on the corner of Maple Avenue and Spring Street. When I bought my first record player in the mid-1950s, I spent hours at C.B. Ellis Music Store perusing its large selection of 45-rpm records of my favorite rock-and-roll tunes. This fascinating store provided a soundproof booth where you could listen to records before you purchased them.

We sometimes ate lunch at Zack's on the corner of Front and Worth Streets. Originally named the Alamance Hot Weiner Lunch, this small restaurant was purchased in 1928 by Zack Touloupas, a Greek immigrant, and soon it became informally known as "Zack's." The Touloupas family officially changed the name to Zack's sometime in the 1950s, remodeled the restaurant in 1960, gradually expanded the menu, and, in 1978, built a new Zack's on the corner of Davis and Worth Streets. Today, the third generation of the Touloupas family continues to operate it as one of the most popular and iconic eateries in Alamance County. When you walk in the front door today, the smell of hamburgers, hot dogs, chili, and onions is still irresistible.

Sometimes we ate at the lunch counter at Woolworth's, one of three dime stores on Main Street (the other two were Rose's and McClellan's). It was always busy. There were only a couple tables for patrons, so most people sat at the long row of stools, while others stood behind them waiting to grab their stools the moment they finished eating. This is where I had my first club sandwich, and I still love them to this day.

We usually shopped until it was time to catch one of the last buses or trains back to Mebane that night. The walk from the Mebane bus station

Above: Alamance Hot Weiner Lunch, 1952. *Courtesy of Don Bolden.*

Left: Three generations at Zack's. *Courtesy of Zack Touloupas.*

The Dentzel Carousel has long been one of Burlington City Park's favorite attractions. *Courtesy of Don Bolden.*

The Melville Dairy Bar was a favorite destination for milk shake and ice cream lovers year round. *Courtesy of the Scott Collection.*

home added to the growing fatigue, especially when we were loaded down with packages or when it was rainy and windy, but it didn't detract from the day's happiness.

Sometimes on Saturday and Sunday, we'd spend a long afternoon at Burlington City Park. As a child, I loved to ride the famous and beautiful Dentzel Carousel, built in the early 1900s and purchased by the City of Burlington in 1948 from an amusement park in Ohio. Equally enjoyable was the ride on the Kiwanis Special, a miniature train that traveled over a circular track through woods, over a small stream, and through a tunnel. We also attended Fourth of July fireworks and picnics at the park.

As I got older, I sometimes played tennis at Burlington City Park or went swimming in the outdoor pool at the adjacent YMCA. We usually topped off a day at the park with a trip to the nearby Melville Dairy Bar for a delicious sandwich and milk shake.

Chapter 10
ELEMENTARY SCHOOL DAYS

My parents first began to prepare me for school in the summer of 1947, when they took me to downtown Mebane to buy school clothes at Jones' Department Store and classroom supplies at Rose's dime store. The shopping trip also included a visit to the Mebane Clinic to get the necessary preschool shots for childhood diseases, including the vaccine for smallpox, which in 1947 was still a danger even in western nations like the United States.

I entered Mebane School two years after the end of World War II. A faded two-story brick building with a classroom and gymnasium annex, the school and grounds occupied an entire block on the corner of Jackson and Third Streets just two blocks from the center of town. During this southern era of "separate but equal," it was open only to white students. Black students attended an inferior elementary school in the West End section of Mebane. Dual elementary and high school systems were the rule throughout Alamance County.

Mebane School always had a distinctive aroma, a mingling of chalk, waxy or oily wooden floors, white library paste, and books. Radiators along the outside walls struggled to keep the big rooms with the high ceilings warm during cold weather, while in the early fall and spring, the wide, tall windows were opened to let in the fresh air and cool breezes. At the back of the room was a long, shallow closet where we hung our jackets or sweaters and stored our lunches, book satchels, galoshes, baseball gloves, and other playground equipment.

Above: A side view of Mebane School in the 1940s. *Courtesy of Mebane Historical Museum.*

Left: The author all dressed up for his first grade school photo. *Courtesy of the author.*

On the corner across the street on one side of the school was the First Baptist Church, and beside it was Clark's Store, a small, run-down wooden building that carried a few groceries and was a favorite hangout for high school boys sneaking a smoke and exchanging dirty stories before school and at lunchtime.

The Teacherage

Many of our teachers had known us since we were born and had taught our older brothers and sisters in the very same classrooms and desks. Until I got to the seventh grade, they were all female. Some had come to Mebane straight out of college, young and single, and married local men and settled down permanently in Mebane, continuing to teach while they raised their families. Others moved on after a year or two to other towns, seeking a better teaching position or a better chance of landing a husband.

If they were single when they moved into town, they often stayed at the Mebane Teacherage, a two-story house on Jackson Street directly across from the Mebane Public School. There were few places for single women to live in Mebane, and the teacherage was convenient, safe, and inexpensive.

The Teacherage could house fourteen teachers at once but usually had fewer than that, which was a good thing since it had only two bathrooms. The teachers shared the rent, utilities, grocery costs, and cooking chores and sometimes entertained dates in the living room. Most didn't have automobiles, so they took the bus to Burlington, Greensboro, or Chapel Hill to shop or go to movies or restaurants. In Mebane, they went to the local theater, ball games at the high school, local drugstores for ice cream and milkshakes, and read or played bridge at night if they weren't grading papers or preparing for classes. Like other teachers at the school, they sometimes went to the homes of sick students to deliver assignments or pick up homework. The principal and the community expected them to go to church on Sunday, and they usually did. Haw River and some other school systems in the county also provided housing for some of their single teachers, but that practice ended in most communities by 1960.

When my class entered the classroom on the first day in 1947, we became part of a group of friends who would go through twelve years of school together, except for the two and a half years that some of us spent at E.M. Yoder Elementary School before rejoining our classmates who

The Haw River Teachery. *Courtesy of the Haw River Historical Museum.*

had remained in the old school building. We formed strong bonds, and we formed them early.

The school was the center of the community and received strong support from citizens who donated their time and money to school activities. In fact, in the little town of just over two thousand people, the entire community was like one big extended family. It has often been said that "it takes an entire village to raise a child." When I was growing up, the town of Mebane carried out that responsibility very, very well.

The principal through all our school years was E.M. Yoder, who held that position at Mebane School from 1935 until the opening of Eastern High School in 1962, when he continued as the principal of Mebane Middle School until entering a well-deserved retirement in 1966. We respected this good and kind man, but we feared him, too, for he sometimes appeared to be gruff and stern. For years, rumors circulated that he kept an electric paddle in his office.

Most of the students at Mebane School were the children of factory workers, downtown storeowners and employees, professional people, and farmers in the surrounding countryside. Boys wore bib overalls or knickers, and girls wore dresses or skirts and blouses. Many students lived close enough to walk or ride bicycles to school, while those from rural areas rode school buses. Some went barefoot in the early grades, and some brought their lunches in brown bags instead of buying hot food from the cafeteria run for many years by Mrs. Fannie Warren. A few walked home for lunch.

When I started school, polio was a threat to us and to children across the nation. We were inoculated against smallpox and other childhood diseases before we entered school, but there was no vaccine for polio. We grew

Mrs. Nelson's second grade class at Mebane Public School, 1948–49. *Courtesy of the author.*

up hearing our parents talk about the disease and seeing photographs in newspapers and magazines of children and adults imprisoned in iron lungs or struggling to walk with heavy braces. No wonder it was the most feared childhood disease in the nation.

North Carolina experienced several polio epidemics over the years, with the worst one coming in the summer of 1948, when we were enjoying the break between the first and second grades. It was so bad that the Alamance County Board of Health banned all children under the age of sixteen from churches, movie theaters, swimming pools, and other public gatherings. The opening day for county schools was delayed for two weeks, as was the beginning of high school football practice and games.

In September, the number of new cases began its expected decline, so on September 11, the ban on public gatherings of children was lifted. When the epidemic ended, Alamance County had registered fifty-three new cases for the year, and North Carolina had led the nation with 2,500 new cases and over one hundred deaths. The polio fears subsided briefly but resurfaced in

A Haw River polio victim in the late 1940s. *Courtesy of Haw River Historical Museum.*

future years until Jonas Salk's vaccine was introduced in 1955 and succeeded in eradicating the disease in just a few years.

In the first few grades in school, we memorized the alphabet and sat in groups learning to read. Like millions of other American students, our reading instruction relied heavily on the "Dick and Jane" books that dominated the market for decades. This series used the whole word approach (also called the "look-say" method) rather than the phonics approach. Featuring stories about things typical first graders did, it employed pictures, big print, short words and simple sentences, a simple but gradually expanding vocabulary, word recognition, and repetition—all designed to teach us to recognize words and understand their meaning in context.

Only a few pages long, the books contained phrases like "Look, look," "Come, Dick, come and see," and "Stop, Sally." I don't remember ever thinking as I read these that my family and friends did not talk this way. I also did not have a dog, a cat, two younger sisters, or a father who wore a suit to work, and there wasn't a white picket fence around our house. But I never really thought about those things either. I learned to read from these books, and I suppose I unconsciously picked up the values in them or had my own similar values reinforced by them.

The Dick and Jane books depicted an ideal white, middle-class family and an ideal childhood. The major characters were Father, Mother, three children (Dick, Jane, and Sally), doting grandparents who lived on a farm, a dog (Spot), and an orange kitten (Puff). Father was a happy, smiling, successful businessman who wore a suit and hat to work and came home every afternoon to play with his children. Mother was a good wife and homemaker who was always working around the house yet always had time to play with the children. Neighbors were friendly and helpful, and the milkman and dry cleaners made deliveries to the front door.

The whole family lived a happy, white, ideal life in a world of their own, uncomplicated by the problems of the outside world. The books taught the values of white, middle-class suburban families of the 1940s and 1950s—stable families, a father who worked and a mother who stayed at home with the children, love and respect for parents and other adults, personal responsibility, cooperation with others, encouragement of others, and the values of wholesome fun and play. Children were happy and never had to worry about anything. Often criticized for portraying an unrealistic and unrepresentative view of the world, the Dick and Jane books had taught reading and wholesome values to close to 85 million children by the time the series ended in the 1970s.

In the early grades, we learned the three R's along with history, geography, art, and health. We learned about the world outside Mebane and Alamance County from the *Weekly Reader*, made leaf and bird scrapbooks, gave current events, exchanged Valentines, decorated the room for Thanksgiving and Christmas, and sang Christmas carols. We wrote on Blue Horse notebook paper and Write-Rite tablets with pencils or fountain pens (ball points had been introduced in 1945, but they didn't work very well). We bought delicious Dreamsicles, Fudgesicles, and Brown Mules at a window in the cafeteria after lunch and had—or wanted to have—boyfriends or girlfriends. We became accustomed to the school bell tolling the beginning and end of the school day and to the little bell that signaled that Mr. Yoder was about to make an announcement over the intercom.

As we got older, the days began with the pledge of allegiance to the flag, a Bible reading, and a prayer. In some classes, the teacher went around the room calling on everyone to say a Bible verse for the day. "Jesus wept" was the one said most often, and the earliest.

My love of reading naturally led me down the road to bibliophilism. Like so many other boys my age, the first books I collected were comic books. I was introduced to them by my sisters, who read me stories about "The Fox and the Crow" and other animals in *Real Screen Comics* and other comics before I was old enough to read. When I began to read them myself, I began to collect and to trade them. After I had read the ones I bought, I would pile them in my bike basket and ride across town to trade books with my friends. It was like we had our own lending library, pooling our resources so we could read more comic books than we could afford alone.

I was willing to trade my copies of *Looney Tunes* and *Superman*, but for years I saved all my copies of *Walt Disney's Comics and Stories*, *Uncle Scrooge*, and other Disney comics. I bought most of my comics at the drugstores downtown, but I subscribed to *Walt Disney's Comics and Stories* so I wouldn't risk missing a single issue. It was my first magazine subscription, and by paying one dollar a year for twelve issues (each advertising fifty-two full pages for only ten cents), I could save twenty cents, guarantee that I wouldn't miss a single issue, and enjoy the anticipation of waiting for them to arrive in the mail. I kept copies of these issues, along with the *Sporting News* and *Sport* magazine, in boxes under my bed for several years until silverfish found them and my mother made me put these treasures in the trash.

In the early '50s, I left these comics behind for *The Crypt of Terror*, *The Vault of Horror*, and other gruesome comics put out by E.C. Comics, one of the giants in the business. My parents didn't like for me to read these, and neither did many educators, psychiatrists and congressmen, who attacked them as lurid, provocative books that encouraged children to commit violent, even criminal acts. The public outcry caused the comic book industry to adopt a Comics Code designed to tone down the violence in order to deflect congressional regulation. Many comics folded, and comic book sales declined dramatically after years of booming sales. By then, I was getting too old for most comic books, except for *Classics Illustrated* and *Mad* magazine.

Comic book adaptations of great works of literature, the *Classics Illustrated* series appeared in the mid-1940s. They reached their height of popularity in the early 1950s before waning in the face of mass paperbacks and television. It was in these comic book pages that I had my first introduction to *The Iliad*, *Les Misérables*, *Moby Dick*, and other literary classics. I found the stories fascinating and convinced myself that I was really learning about the great works of literature. I didn't know that contemporary literary critics claimed that the books distorted the plot and concentrated on bloody, gory, and violent scenes. I did know as I moved into the middle grades and high school that English teachers condemned them as superficial adaptations of great literature that caused a decline in reading skills by providing an easy escape from the hard work of reading the originals. I also knew that I'd better not bring them to class and that some teachers were better than others in detecting book reports written from the comic books rather than from the original works.

I soon discovered *Mad* magazine, which first appeared in 1952 as a satirical comic book spoofing television, the movies, politics, magazine advertisements and television commercials, and even other comic books. When the 1954 Comics Code drove many horror and war and crime comics out of business, *Mad* survived and prospered by changing to a magazine format priced at twenty-five cents an issue so it wouldn't be subjected to the new comics code. It was very successful, delighting many adolescents and adults with its clever, irreverent stories on "Superdooperman," "Howdy Dooit," "Mickey Rodent," "Bat Boy," and "Darnold Duck," satirizing everybody and everything.

As I progressed through elementary school, I read the usual books for my age group in the school library and public library. Like most boys, I enjoyed *Treasure Island* and other adventure books by Robert Louis Stevenson, and I bought copies of *Treasure Island* and *Kidnapped*, which took their place on my small bookshelf alongside Tom Meany's biographies of Babe Ruth and Bob Feller as the first books I ever owned. I also owned several Mark Twain novels, and in the sixth grade I played Tom Sawyer in a school play about Tom and Huck whitewashing the fence.

Not long after I started the first grade, Mother took me to the Mebane Public Library to get a library card. The librarian, Myrtle Miles, gave me the card along with a serious lecture on the importance of taking care of the books I checked out and returning them on time. Like the school library, the public library nourished my love of books and reading and served as a gateway to the world outside of Alamance County.

Fear of the Russians and Communism

Without really knowing anything about it, I grew up knowing that communism was bad because my parents and teachers said that it was. The Korean War began in 1950 when I was nine years old, before we or many other Americans had television. At the time, I didn't know where Korea was or what the war was all about.

Too young to follow and understand most of what was going on in the Cold War, I nevertheless knew Russia and communist China were our enemies, that communism was an evil system threatening to take over our world, that we were in a nuclear arms race and all the atomic tests were polluting the air with radiation, and that if the Russians used atomic weapons against us, we might all die.

Our teachers talked about it and showed maps of what one H-bomb could do to a city the size of New York or Washington. *Time*, *Life*, and other popular magazines of the day often featured cover stories on the "red menace" posed by Joe Stalin, Mao Zedong, and other communist rulers. We worried occasionally, but most of the time we put it in the backs of our minds and convinced ourselves that war with Russia and China really wouldn't happen and that even if it did our government would win and take care of us.

The bomb also helped spark the growth in science fiction novels and movies about space battles, invasions from outer space, and monsters created by radioactive mutations. Then, in 1957, Nevil Shute published *On the Beach*, a best-selling novel that depicted the coming extinction of the world after a mutually destructive atomic war between Russia and the United States. It was made into a powerful motion picture at the end of the decade.

Desegregation

In May 1954, as I was finishing the seventh grade, the Supreme Court handed down its *Brown v. the Board of Education* decision outlawing segregation in public schools. It aroused a storm of protest all across the South, and in Mebane, it was naturally the talk of the day in town and among the teachers and students in the schools. At the time, Alamance County had fifteen white schools and seven black schools. The total enrollment was about ten thousand, almost evenly split between city and county.

But in the fall of 1954, when my class at E.M. Yoder moved back across town to Mebane School, we began the eighth grade in a school system destined to remain segregated for almost another decade.

Chapter 11
PAPERBOYS AND A GIRL NAMED HAZEL

When I was about thirteen years old, I got a job as a paperboy. It was a dream job. Being a paperboy (there were few papergirls anywhere then, and certainly none in Mebane) carried a certain amount of status, signaling that you were mature, responsible, and ambitious. There weren't many ways for boys twelve or thirteen years old to make money, and I thought the ones that were available, like raking leaves or mowing lawns, required too much work and did not provide a steady income. Only about a half dozen Mebane boys were lucky enough to land a paper route, and I was fortunate to become a carrier for the morning *Greensboro Daily News* rather than the *Burlington Daily Times-News,* which, as an afternoon paper, would interfere with my time on the baseball diamond or basketball court.

My day began around 5:45 a.m. when I peddled my bike to the loading platform at the Mebane Post Office to wait along with several other carriers for our newspapers to arrive by truck from Greensboro. When they came, I cut the wire around my newspaper bundle, folded or rolled up the papers so they could be thrown from my bike, and loaded them into the canvas bag in my bike basket. I loved the smell of fresh newsprint, and even today the scent of a crisp newspaper is second only to coffee as my favorite morning aroma. After taking a quick glance at the sports pages, I rode off to deliver my sixty or so papers along a route that stretched for several miles.

It was fun, not work. It seemed like just a nice bike ride through my little hometown in the quiet predawn hours. I enjoyed the camaraderie with other paperboys and the challenge of throwing the paper in exactly the right spot on doorsteps and porches. Unfortunately, I once lost a customer because I broke the glass in his front storm door when the paper sailed a little off target. My route took me over a large portion of town, from the houses and apartments of the poor to the finest homes in town. I was usually home by 7:00 a.m. and ready for a big breakfast after an hour's bike ride.

Hostile dogs and bad winter weather were the major drawbacks to the job. I was often chased by dogs and was once bitten by one on a dark winter morning, and snow and ice storms made riding a bike with a heavy load of newspapers downright hazardous. But my worst experience during the three years I worked as a carrier came in the fall of 1954, when I got caught in the wind and rain in advance of Hurricane Hazel's surprise midday journey through the middle of the state.

The around-the-clock hurricane watches of today are a far cry from the time Hurricane Hazel hit the North Carolina coast. In the early 1950s, residents of inland North Carolina paid little attention to hurricanes, which occurred rarely and even then usually inflicted their damage mainly on coastal areas. It wasn't until 1953 that the U.S. Weather Bureau began using women's names to identify and track tropical storms and hurricanes. There were no weather satellites, Doppler radar systems, computer models, or other sophisticated detection and warning devices like we're accustomed to today, and at a time when many people still didn't own a television set, there were no television journalists standing on a beach in the midst of a roaring storm reporting on how bad conditions were.

Then, in the mid-1950s, North Carolina was hit by a rash of storms, seven hurricanes in two years. Hurricane Hazel was by far the worst, and it's one I've never forgotten.

Hazel began as a low-pressure system in the tropical Atlantic and was first identified on October 5, near Grenada. From then on, the U.S. Weather Bureau in Miami tracked the storm with radar and weather planes and gave daily reports of its trek toward the eastern coast of the United States. Forecasters eventually posted storm warnings from Charleston, South Carolina, to the Virginia Capes and predicted that the storm would move very close to Cape Hatteras as it headed up the coast.

Around six o'clock on the morning of Friday, October 15, I rode my bike to the Mebane Post Office in a heavy rain to pick up my newspapers. As I started out on my route, it began to rain so hard that I could barely see the road, and the wind blew my bike over twice, dumping my papers in the wet street. Pretty soon I was wet to the bone, and the papers in my canvas newspaper bag were soaked. I could hardly see to ride, but I kept on, determined to finish my route.

When I returned home, my parents had heard on the radio that the storm was going to hit on the coast somewhere near the North Carolina–South Carolina border. I changed clothes, ate breakfast and walked to school, never thinking that our little town, close to 180 miles from the coast, could be in harm's way.

Meanwhile, conditions worsened. The eye of the storm came inland over the Brunswick County islands between 9:30 and 10:00 a.m., with winds gusting to 150 miles an hour at Calabash, and the word soon spread that the storm was moving farther westward than anticipated and that the winds had reached 100 miles an hour in Raleigh. Relatives and friends called one another to make sure that they had heard that the storm was heading inland and that they had better get prepared.

In Alamance County, as in other areas, school officials were caught off guard. The storm had not been expected to move into our area, and when it did, it moved quickly. Alamance County school officials decided to let schools out shortly after 1:00 p.m. at the height of the storm. Students quickly boarded buses, were picked up by their parents, or began the wet and windy walk home. I was drenched by the time I had made it only a few steps outside the school, and I fought the wind and rain for six blocks, walking and running and trying to find my way through the blinding rain.

I finally made it home, where my mother and I huddled in the center of the house and hoped the storm wouldn't rip off our roof or bring the big trees in our yard crashing down on our house. The wind and rain continued for several hours and then let up as the storm passed over us in its rapid rush northward, moving at fifty miles an hour and cutting a broad path of destruction through the mid-Atlantic states, the Northeast, and Canada, eventually crossing the Arctic Circle and dying out in Scandinavia.

When the storm was over, we went outside to survey the damage. The yard was covered in several inches of water and littered with debris from our trees. It was the same all up and down the street. Across town, power was out for several hours, many trees were down, and a few roofs were damaged, but otherwise Mebane escaped with minor damage. So did the rest of Alamance County, though the storm did destroy the third-story roof of the W.J. Nicks General Merchandise store in Graham.

The storm devastated North Carolina's southern beaches. Statewide, wind and floods destroyed some fifteen thousand houses and other buildings, damaged thirty-nine thousand others, leveled thousands of trees, and caused power outages that lasted for days. Over two hundred people were injured, and nineteen were killed. All told, nearly one hundred people were killed in the United States by the storm, along with over five hundred others in the storm's path. Hazel was such an unusual event that the following day, many people from Alamance County and other inland areas drove to the beaches to see the destruction, but they were turned away at the outskirts by the National Guard, the North Carolina State Highway Patrol, and other authorities.

The only positive side of Hazel was that it ended a severe drought in the Piedmont that had forced Mebane town officials to import water in tanker trucks. Friday afternoon's edition of the *Burlington Daily Times-News* headlined "Rain Definitely Ends County Water Shortage" and reported that the Alamance County area had close to six inches of rain.

Hurricane Hazel was the only Category 4 hurricane to strike North Carolina in the twentieth century. For a long time, until Hugo hit in 1989 and Fran in 1996, Hazel was the one everybody talked about, the one all others were compared to, and the one that taught North Carolinians that it's not just coastal dwellers who need to cast a wary eye toward storms that form in the warm waters of the Atlantic every year between June 1 and November 30.

My years as a paperboy also brought my first introduction to American capitalism. I inherited a route with about fifty-five customers, and by canvassing the homes in my territory, I built it up to over sixty so I could increase my income. Of the forty cents a week each customer paid me for weekly and Sunday deliveries, twenty-eight went to the newspaper company and the rest came to me. I usually collected from my customers on Fridays and Saturdays, duly noting their payment in my green account book as we made small talk at their door. Some left their payment under a flowerpot or welcome mat on the porch in case they weren't home when I came to collect. I always looked forward to Christmas, when I usually received about sixty dollars in tips, a princely sum in my eyes.

My paper route taught me valuable lessons about responsibility, time and money management, diligence, and dealing with a wide variety of people. It was a job that I had to do every day, 365 days a year. Thanks to the seven to eight dollars I earned each week, I was able to open a savings account at the bank, purchase a new Firestone bike on credit (paying one dollar a week until it was paid off), and buy baseball equipment, Topps baseball cards, school clothing, and books.

Times changed. The demise of most afternoon papers and the rise of adults covering large newspaper routes in automobiles put most adolescent and teenage carriers out of work. The last carrier who brought my paper on a bicycle was a papergirl (Sarah Bright) who delivered the afternoon *Lexington Dispatch* when I was living there in the 1970s. Since I've moved to Mebane, I've never seen the early bird who throws both my *Greensboro News and Record* and *Burlington Times-News* papers onto my driveway as he drives by. I pay for both by sending annual checks to the circulation offices.

Most newspaper readers today probably don't lament the disappearance of paperboys, but many young people are missing out on a great experience from a simpler time when America still resembled the nation portrayed in Norman Rockwell's paintings on the covers of the old *Saturday Evening Post.*

Chapter 12

HIGH SCHOOL YEARS

In 1955, we entered high school in the midst of what would later be called the Fabulous Fifties and the Nifty Fifties. A popular general and grandfatherly figure, Dwight Eisenhower, was in the White House. The nation was experiencing unprecedented prosperity, high employment, low inflation, an outpouring of consumer goods, and the continued movement of television into almost every home in America. A nationwide polio vaccine campaign was inoculating millions of children against that dreaded disease. The nation was at peace, for the Korean War had ended over two years earlier, and few people were paying any attention to America's growing interest and involvement in the little country of Vietnam so many thousands of miles away. We still worried about the Russians, the Chinese, thermonuclear weapons, supersonic bombers, and nuclear missiles, but we gradually put these concerns in the backs of our minds and focused on enjoying the teenage life.

At Mebane High School, we were about sixty students out of a total enrollment of a little over two hundred. We were the largest freshman class in the history of the school, but behind us in the lower grades was the first wave of baby boomers, part of the nationwide population explosion that was already crowding schools and creating a teacher shortage. E.M. Yoder Elementary School was already overcrowded, so South Mebane Elementary would be built in 1957, and in 1962, students from Mebane High School would be combined with students from Haw River and Pleasant Grove to form the new Eastern High School.

Mebane High School was still made up entirely of white students and white teachers. The only black faces on the campus belonged to the custodian, James, a beloved figure who had been with the school for as long as most people could remember; his wife; and some of the young women who worked in the school cafeteria.

For many students in the rest of the South, the years spent in high school were crowded with racial tensions, confrontations, and violence—murders, shootings, bombings, and the burning of schools, churches, and homes of civil rights activists. Luckily, we had no serious incidents in our town or our school.

Teenagers

Students entering high school in 1955 were part of the largest young generation up until that time. Nationwide, there were 16.5 million teenagers, a term that first appeared in the 1940s but did not come into wide currency until the mid-1950s. We were, as a *Life* magazine article called us in 1956, a "generation in a spotlight" because there were so many of us and because we were developing a subculture that set us apart from our parents and even from the college-age students just a few years older than us. Thanks to the affluence of that decade, passed on to us through parental allowances and our part-time jobs, we had more money to spend than any generation before us, and we spent it on phonograph records, movies, clothing, cars, and other consumer goods. Our subculture spread through movies, music, television shows and especially the medium of advertising that latched on to the lucrative teen market. We thought we were something special; after all, there was so much about us in the newspapers and magazines and on television and the radio.

Slang

We developed our own slang, sometimes borrowed from older generations and modified—such as "wheels," "hot rod," "passion pit" (drive-in theaters), "see you later alligator," and "knockers"—or from the music and beatnik world: "hip," "chick," "square," "cool," and "dig." We had our slang for sex—"going all the way," "doing the deed," "coming across," "horny," and "hot"—as well as pejorative descriptions like "fink," "drag," "dumb cluck," "loser," and "out-to-lunch." A bad joke would provoke a sarcastic "Hardeeharhar," and the sight of a sexy girl would elicit cries of, "Hubba, hubba!"

Music, Idols, and Dress

We acquired our own music, the rock-and-roll music that appeared in the mid-1950s, and our own idols: Pat Boone, Elvis Presley, Ricky Nelson, and others just a little older or even our own age, as well as James Dean and other movie stars and Mickey Mantle and other athletes.

By the time we got to high school, the music we were listening and dancing to was undergoing a radical change. Although we still liked some of the music our older siblings and parents listened to—such as Perry Como, Frank Sinatra, Patti Page, Doris Day, and others—our ears were beginning to like the rock-and-roll sound that was making its way into the world of white teenagers and onto our 45-rpm record players.

As our high school years progressed, rock-and-roll music steadily became more and more a part of our lives. While some of the singers were white (Elvis Presley, Ricky Nelson, Pat Boone, Buddy Holly, Jerry Lee Lewis, and others), increasingly, the tunes we listened and danced to were performed by black musicians like Fats Domino, Little Richard, Chuck Berry, Sam Cooke, the Platters, and the Coasters. We did not care what color they were as long as they kept churning out that music with the rock-and-roll beat.

Elvis Presley appeared at a show at Williams High School in the mid-1950s. In the *Burlington Times-News* on August 18, 2013, managing editor Jay Ashley wrote that "I first heard about Elvis from my aunt, who saw him at a show at Williams High School in the mid-1950s. She told me he dressed in a lime-green sports coat. Elvis stayed at the Piedmont Hotel downtown because it was less expensive than the Alamance Hotel. He ate at the Brightwood Inn, and they still decorate a booth out there in his honor."

All across the nation, many among the older generation condemned rock-and-roll as a dangerous new music that undermined morality, promoted teen sexual activity, threatened Christianity, and encouraged an unhealthy mixing of the races. But it spread to Mebane with little fanfare. Iris Abernathy bought the latest rock tunes for the Teenage Club; the Mebane Theater showed *Blackboard Jungle* with its pioneering theme song "Rock Around the Clock," which had precipitated rioting in some big cities, with few objections from the local community; and teens played it at parties held in the basements or garages of their parents' homes without any apparent ill effects.

Although we loved rock-and-roll, we never abandoned the crooners and ballad singers like Perry Como and the newer ones like the Everly Brothers, Johnny Mathis, Pat Boone, Bobby Darin, the Fleetwoods, and Nat King Cole. Many of us listened to these and to older romantic tunes on the popular Raleigh radio station WPTF-FM, where smooth-talking Jimmy Capps played requests on his *Our Best to You* beginning at 11:05 p.m. from Monday through Friday.

Dress

Teens adopted a wide range of fashions, many of them copied from young males on *American Bandstand*, *The Adventures of Ozzie and Harriet*, and other television shows. Boys sported crew cut or flattop haircuts and wore V-neck sweaters, loafers or white bucks, turned-up collars, tight pegged pants, denim jeans with rolled-up cuffs, narrow belts, black slacks with a buckle in the back, and pink shirts. "Greasers," and they were scarce at Mebane and other Alamance County high schools, wore black leather jackets, T-shirts with cigarette packs carried in a rolled-up sleeve, and ducktail haircuts. Teenage girls wore ponytails and poodle cuts, skirts and blouses, dresses, blazers, short shorts, rolled-up jeans with blouses or men's shirts, loafers, and brown and white saddle shoes. Athletes and cheerleaders wore coats or sweaters embellished with a gold "M" or other monogram denoting their high school.

Gunsmoke, *The Mickey Mouse Club*, and *The Honeymooners* were among the television premiers that fall, joining *The $64,000 Question*, *Disneyland*, *I Love Lucy*, and other popular returning shows. Fall moviegoers were leaving their television sets long enough to drop into local movie houses to see *Mr. Roberts*, *The Seven Year Itch*, *Marty*, and other films.

For most of us, growing up young and white in Mebane and other Alamance County towns was pretty easy. There was little crime or juvenile delinquency and no juvenile gangs like those making headlines in large cities like New York and Los Angeles. Drinking and smoking were fairly common among older high school males, but few girls smoked or drank. And although we knew about dope (marijuana, heroin, and cocaine), that was something taken by musicians or beatniks in cities far away from Mebane and other Alamance County towns.

Teenage Clubs

Popular Mebane High School science teacher and Teenage Club director Iris Abernathy. *Courtesy of the author.*

In Burlington, Mebane, and some of the other Alamance County towns, the school system or civic clubs provided safe and convenient hangouts for the teenage population. In the 1940s and '50s, the Burlington Teenage Club met in a room over the police department on Andrews Street. In Mebane, the favorite teen social center was the Crow's Nest Club, generally just called the Teenage Club, which met one night a week from 7:30 p.m. to 10:00 p.m. The club was sponsored by the Junior Women's Club, and the director was our high school science teacher, Iris Abernathy.

Open to all white teenagers in the Mebane schools, membership was only twenty-five cents a year. Members had to agree to follow strict written rules—no drinking, gambling, smoking, or profanity—and had to conduct themselves "as ladies and gentlemen at all times." Once a week, teenagers climbed one flight of stairs to a large room over Rose's for several hours of teenage fun—playing ping-pong or card games and talking, flirting, and dancing to the latest teenage hits or golden oldies played on an old Wurlitzer jukebox. We enjoyed a wide range of dances, including slow dance, rock-and-roll, square dances, the stroll, and the bunny hop. In our senior year, I was one of several members of the Teenage Club chosen to appear on Ty Boyd's televised *Dance Party* on WTVD in nearby Durham.

On dates, we went to ballgames, homecoming dances, the Junior-Senior Banquet, the Fall Festival, the May Day festival, and other school functions. We cruised around, often stopping at drive-in restaurants like Huey's and the A&M Grill in Mebane, Allen's in Haw River, Hunter's or Skid's in Burlington, or the Boar and Castle in Greensboro. We bowled

The 1956 Mebane High School May Day Court poses in the gymnasium. *Courtesy of the author.*

Opposite: A 1950s advertisement for the Haw River Movie Theater. *Courtesy of the Haw River Historical Museum.*

at Roy's Bowling Center in Burlington, went to the State Theater or Paramount Theater in Burlington, to the Haw River Theater, and to the East 70 Drive-In and the new putt-putt golf course on Highway 70. Some dating couples went steady, as the language of the time described it, which meant that they were really, really serious and that both were off limits to others.

Most of the time, I cruised or dated with a male friend who had a car. Gasoline was cheap—less than thirty cents a gallon, I think—so when we went cruising, several of us would pile into one car, pool our money to give to the driver, and then ride, sometimes for hours.

It was permissible in our high school culture to date girls from any place out of town—in fact, this carried some prestige, seeming to be more exotic or romantic—except those from Mebane's major sports rival, Haw River.

We had a curious double standard: it was okay for us to date girls from other towns, but we deeply resented boys from these towns coming in and dating our girls. The enmity between Haw River "River Rats" and the Mebane "Polecats" went back decades.

Drive-In Theaters

For real privacy, when we wanted to be alone for some serious necking, we parked—sometimes on lonely roads but more often in the safety of the drive-in theater. However, if we were afraid of running into some of our friends who would spread the news that we were at that passion pit, we went to some other passion pit in some other town.

Drive-in theaters first appeared during the Depression years and then exploded across the country in the late 1940s and 1950s through their appeal to young married couples with children and others who found indoor theaters to be too inconvenient, expensive, or confining. To young dating couples, these "passion pits with pix," as some dubbed them, provided far more privacy and opportunities for intimacy than the balconies of downtown indoor theaters patrolled by suspicious ushers. Many dating couples found the drive-ins to be irresistible, in spite of the sullied reputations they might acquire (especially the girls) if they went there too often. On Friday and Saturday nights, prime dating nights, long lines formed at the East 70 Drive-In on North Church Street in Burlington or the Circle-G Drive-In on Ossippee Road as couples came early hoping to get parking spots as near the back row as possible. The drive-ins typically featured horror movies, teen flicks, and standard movies that had exhausted their run in indoor theaters.

Sputnik

On Friday, October 4, 1957, as we were settling into our junior year, the Soviet Union sent the first artificial satellite, *Sputnik*, into orbit over five hundred miles above the earth. Although it was only twenty-two inches in diameter and weighed only 184 pounds, it sent shock waves all across the planet and especially through the United States.

The Soviet feat was the talk of the nation and our school for several days, and very quickly the attention began to focus on education. The media and some of our teachers told us that the Soviet accomplishment showed the superiority of the Russian educational system, particularly in the areas of science and mathematics. We read in the newspapers and heard on television or from our teachers that American schools needed to beef up their curriculum, adding more math, science, and foreign languages, and that students needed to study harder. There was a blitz of newspaper and magazine articles and books about the "crisis in education," "the Cold War in the classrooms," and the pressing need for major reforms.

All across the country in our last two years in high school, federal and state governments poured money into education, upgrading teacher training, raising standards, revising curricula, building new schools, and consolidating many small secondary schools into large comprehensive high schools with better laboratories, a larger selection of courses, and better-trained teachers. With only two years left in our high school career, it was too late for us to benefit from these reforms. *Sputnik* was a wake-up call for American education, but the military threat and educational crisis were overblown, and the panic over *Sputnik* and the educational and missile gaps slowly subsided.

It is difficult now for us to remember what we studied and learned in high school. Some of us can remember agonizing over math problems, sitting day after day while we took turns reading aloud from a Shakespeare play or *Silas Marner* in English class, being warned by our English teachers not to get our book reports from *Classics Illustrated*, writing our book reports from *Classics Illustrated*, working on the big senior English term paper, being part of the first class of Mebane High School students to take a course (American history, taught by Lois Edinger) over the new UNC-TV station, having three different math teachers in one year, going to the cafeteria for lunch and sitting at the same table every day with the same group of friends, and waiting in great anticipation every year for our yearbooks.

Sports

The late 1940s and 1950s were the waning years of the intense rivalries between the small Alamance County high schools before their identities vanished under the school consolidation efforts of the 1960s. While the "big-city schools" of Burlington and Graham had more students, larger athletic budgets, and the prestige of playing at higher levels of competition, the high schools serving the rural communities and small mill towns scattered across the county struggled to find enough players and uniforms for interscholastic sports at the Class A level. Some were too small to support a football team, but most were able to field a baseball team and boys' and girls' basketball teams.

The football games were played on rocky fields that usually doubled as baseball diamonds, and heated basketball battles were fought in drafty cracker boxes constructed during the Depression or war years, when financial resources were scarce. The backboards were wooden, and most players saw glass backboards for the first time when they played in the county tournament in the Elon College gymnasium.

High school basketball was in a transition period in the mid-1950s. While the long two-handed set shot and one-handed push shot were still standard

Mebane High School Marching Band, 1950s. *Courtesy of Mebane Historical Museum.*

offensive weapons, more and more teams were imitating professional and college basketball's emphasis on the fast break and one-handed jump shot. But slam dunks were practically nonexistent, and the final scores of games were generally much lower than those of today, though the 1956–57 championship Mebane team averaged 79.4 points per game during the regular season and scored over 90.0 points twice, while holding their opponents to an average of 55.0 points per contest.

The girls' game was showing no sign of impending changes. Operating under the assumption that females were the weaker sex and should not exert themselves like their male counterparts on the court, the girls' game still was essentially a half-court game. Each team had six players—three forwards and three guards—and players could take only three dribbles before they had to pass and were prohibited from crossing the half-court line. They were supposed to act like ladies at all times.

In the mid-1950s, Mebane and the other county schools in the Class A Alamance County Conference—Haw River, Eli Whitney, Altamahaw-Ossipee, Alexander Wilson, Pleasant Grove, Sylvan, Elon, and E.M. Holt—carried on fierce basketball rivalries that were closely followed by their small student bodies and local communities. Graduates of the schools, especially if they continued to live in their hometown, were fanatical supporters of their old high school. Rivalries generated high emotions, and arguments between fans from opposing teams sometimes escalated into fistfights behind the bleachers or in the small parking lots.

Mebane's biggest rival in football and basketball was the little school of Haw River, just a few miles up Highway 70. We always felt that Mebane was a bigger, more sophisticated town and that our high school was far superior to the one in Haw River. The games between the two little schools usually brought out the best in the players and sometimes the worst in the fans.

The Mebane gym was packed for most games, especially when hated rivals like the Haw River Indians or Alexander Wilson Eagles were in town, and the roar of the crowd in such confined quarters was deafening. The crowd was so near the court and the bleachers were so small that players could easily pick out friends, relatives, or hecklers anywhere in the gym. Opposing players could be intimidated in such an atmosphere, and so could referees, who wisely kept an eye on the nearest exit when their calls went against the Tigers. One referee, Jack McKeon, the popular catcher and, later, manager for the Burlington Bees and eventually the Florida Marlins and several other major-league teams, had to be escorted from the gym by the police after one call against the always guiltless Mebane Tigers.

Right: Jack McKeon was a colorful catcher and manager for the Pirates in the 1950s. *Courtesy of Don Bolden.*

Below: Mebane High School basketball team, 1958–59. *Courtesy of the author.*

The boys' and girls' teams rode the school activity bus to away games. The ride was as much fun as the games themselves, especially when we stopped by the Donut Dinette on North Church Street in Burlington after the game for hamburgers and the best donuts I've ever eaten.

During our high school years, the football team, coached by Archie Walker, won four consecutive Mid-State Conference championships and twice was runner-up for the state Class A title. In the 1956–57 school year, the football team won twelve straight before losing to Edenton in the finals. In that same year, Coach George Shackelford's boys' basketball team won twenty-eight straight games and defeated the Jonesville Blue Jays for the state Class A title. I saw most of the games from the bench. The 1956–1957 Tigers were led by junior center Gene Compton, who, at six-foot-six, towered over most of the other players in the conference in an era when high school players this tall were rare. The girls' basketball team, also coached by Shackelford, had a 19-2 record.

A big step up from our Class A sports were the AAA Burlington High School Bulldogs and the AA Graham Red Devils. In 1951, Burlington High School moved from Broad Street, where it had been from 1917 to 1951, to Church Street and assumed the new name of Walter M. Williams High School. Both Burlington and Graham usually put competitive teams on the field. Graham High had a very successful football team under head coach George Heckman, who compiled a record of 129 wins, 62 losses, and 10 ties during his tenure from 1946 through the mid-1960s.

Graduation and Beyond

In the fall of 1958, we entered our senior year in the same building most of us had started our education in twelve years earlier. The building hadn't changed much—it was just older and in greater need of renovation than ever before—but of course in those twelve years we had changed a lot. We were seniors now, and we thought we were big shots, kings of the hill.

In spite of all the change swirling around us in the late 1950s, most of us were still pretty much a conservative, conformist lot. Few of us questioned the racism and sexism of the time, the policies of our national government, or the values our parents and teachers had handed down to us. We paid little attention to the civil rights battles being fought all across the nation or to the growing influence of the beatniks and other dissenters from the American dream. Although the United States had several hundred advisors in South Vietnam, few of us had ever heard of the troubles brewing there or in the Middle East or Africa.

As we began our senior year in 1958, "Born Too Late," "It's All in the Game," "Rockin' Robin," and "To Know Him Is to Love Him" were playing on our radio stations and record players. The number-one song in January 1959 was the Platters' "Smoke Gets in Your Eyes," and in February, three of our favorite singers—Buddy Holly, J.P. Richardson (the Big Bopper), and Ritchie Valens—died when their small plane crashed near Mason City, Iowa.

Soon it was time for the Junior-Senior Prom, held on Friday, April 10, with "A Southern Plantation" as the theme. The dinner, attended by about 150 students and teachers, was served in the school cafeteria by 15 sophomore girls dressed as Negro slaves. Red roses and candles decorated the table.

After dinner, we walked to the dance just a few steps away in the gymnasium, which had been decorated like a southern plantation, complete with an antebellum mansion and a log cabin for the slaves. There were also several sixth graders dressed in colonial clothing and a large mural that had been painted by members of the junior class. The dance music was provided by a regional group called Moon Mullins and the Night Raiders, five guys in sports coats, pegged trousers, string ties, white buck shoes, and haircuts copied from Elvis Presley and the Everly Brothers.

After the Junior-Senior events, the year quickly came to an end with senior term papers, exams, the distribution of yearbooks, the athletic banquet, the election of the May King and Queen (W.Y. Jobe and Martha Ann McLamb), and the ceremonies surrounding graduation. Our twelve-year journey through the Mebane public schools was over.

In September, many Mebane and Alamance County high school graduates began their college careers. Many males headed to the University of North Carolina, NC State, Duke, or one of the numerous private colleges across the state. Females could not attend Carolina or State until their junior years, so they attended the more sheltered state-supported Woman's College in Greensboro or one of the public or private colleges in the state before transferring to State or Carolina.

Chapter 13

CLERKING AND SODA-JERKING AT WARREN'S DRUG STORE

When I turned fifteen, I decided I wanted to get a part-time job in downtown Mebane. I canvassed the retail stores downtown asking for work and finally landed a job at Jones' Department Store, part of a small chain of regional department stores. The pay was forty-five cents an hour, and I worked a full day on Saturdays and occasionally in the afternoons after school.

I eagerly reported to work early on a warm Saturday morning in September, during the peak of the tobacco auction season, when downtown Mebane was crowded with farmers selling their crops and families buying clothing and school supplies for the opening of school. Mr. Lewis, the manager, told me that while I would work anywhere in the store I was needed, my primary responsibility was to put up stock and help customers in the men's department, which was usually very crowded on Saturdays.

I worked at Jones' for several months while I continued to carry newspapers. Then I got a part-time job at Warren's Drug Store, one of three drugstores in town, all within a block of one another and locally owned. The others were the Mebane Drug Company (commonly called Delmar White's or just Delmar's) on Fourth Street and Carolina Drug on Center Street. All three had soda fountains, milk shakes, and hand-dipped ice cream, and Delmar's even sold refrigerators and other appliances.

Warren's was open six days a week from 8:30 a.m. until about 9:30 p.m., as well as on Sunday afternoon and evening. On Sunday, it and the two other drugstores were the only stores open downtown.

Warren's Drug pharmacist Calvin Oakley and customer Ruth Tyson. *Courtesy of Bill Sykes Jr.*

My starting pay at Warren's was sixty cents an hour, which seemed like a big raise over what Jones' was paying, and I had always wanted to work behind the soda fountain at the drugstore. To me, the drugstore job was a dream job, far better than bagging groceries at local grocery stores, working the curb at local drive-in restaurants, or raking leaves and mowing grass, about the only jobs available for boys my age. It was a comfortable, easy, pleasant, even fun place to work. My erratic work schedule forced me to give up my paper route and some of my afternoon sports activities, but I was able to schedule my afternoon and evening hours so that I could attend basketball practice and games and other after-school activities.

The store was owned by Virgil Warren, but Calvin Oakley (no relation to the author) was the manager and chief pharmacist. He became a partner in the store and eventually the owner sometime in the late 1950s. Doug Isaac joined the store in the late 1950s as a second pharmacist.

The first few days I worked at Warren's, I was overwhelmed by all the things I had to learn. There were so many products, so many brands, so much stuff I had never heard of—and I would have to try to talk intelligently about them to adults, many of whom I knew as teachers, parents of my friends, or merchants who worked near the drugstore and came in frequently. But before long, I was telling customers, "This is probably what you need," "I believe you'll like this," or, to put a little authority behind what I was saying, "Calvin often recommends this."

Warren's Drug was a local example of the thousands of independent drugstores that dotted the nation in the 1950s. It was family owned and a real part of the community, the kind of drugstore that dominated the business until the big chains took over. It had an old-fashioned look, with a patterned marble floor, a soda fountain with a marble counter, and three classic round tables with marble tops where customers sat in wooden chairs while they enjoyed their milkshakes, soft drinks, and ice cream. On Saturday and Sunday afternoons, the black-and-white television in the back of the store was usually turned to a football, basketball, or baseball game.

Like the rest of the town, Warren's was segregated. We had no black employees, but we had many black customers who came in to get prescriptions filled or to buy other items. They bought items from the soda fountain, but they knew they couldn't sit down at one of the three tables to place an order or eat or drink whatever they had bought at the soda fountain.

I waited on customers anywhere in the store, but my main duty was to man the soda fountain. Soft drinks cost a nickel, ice cream cones were six cents for one scoop and twelve cents for two, milkshakes and nut sundaes were twenty-five cents, banana splits were thirty-five cents, and fresh-squeezed orangeades and lemonades were a dime.

In its ads, Warren's billed itself as "Mebane's Best Drug Store," and to me it was. We knew most of our customers by name, let them open charge accounts, and delivered prescriptions and other medicines to people too sick or elderly to come to the store. Calvin and Doug also gave customers good medical advice on using prescriptions and over-the-counter medications.

In the little space available at the front of the store, we carried a wide range of magazines: *Life*, *Look*, the *Saturday Evening Post*, *Time*, *Newsweek*, and other popular photo and article magazines like *Field and Stream*, *Sport*, *Sports Afield*, the *Sporting News*, and *Sports Illustrated*. There was also *True Detective* and *Police Gazette* (which featured stories of drug addicts and criminals and almost a monthly cover story about Hitler being alive in Argentina or some other South American country), as well as *Photoplay*, *Movie Mirror* and other gossip magazines about movie stars, and *True Confessions* and *Modern Romance*. We also carried *Jet* and *Ebony* for our black customers, and something called *Sexology* for the sexually curious.

The magazine rack was conveniently located near the soda fountain, and on slow days or nights, I managed to get in a lot of reading between customers.

It was here that I saw my first *Playboy* magazine. When I first opened it up, I was wild-eyed at the jokes, the stories, and, of course, the "Playmate of the Month" centerfolds. This was much better than the glimpses of the female anatomy in nudist magazines like *Sunshine and Health* and *Modern Sunbathing* that were passed around by our peers who got them from older brothers or had been to a magazine shop on a back street of Burlington.

We sold a little of everything, it seemed. There were long shelves of medicines, including cough syrups; Ben-Gay and other ointments; Lydia Pinkham's Vegetable Compound for "female ailments"; tonics like Geritol, Hadacol, and other products laced with a generous percentage of alcohol and guaranteed to cure a wide range of ailments from "iron deficiency anemia" to insomnia and nervousness and fatigue and so much more; Carter's Little Liver Pills and Doan's Kidney Pills; rock candy (to be mixed with alcoholic drinks for cold cures); and a whole host of other products.

One of the best-selling tonics of the day was Hadacol, a concoction of vitamins, minerals, honey, alcohol (12 percent, listed as a preservative), and several other ingredients. Promoted by its manufacturer as a cure-all for everything from fatigue to high blood pressure, arthritis and allergies, Hadacol was highly advertised on the radio and in magazines and newspapers and was widely sold in drugstores and other retail stores. In 1950, *Time* described it as "a murky brown liquid that tastes something like bilge water, and smells worse." It was condemned by the American Medical Association in 1951, yet it was bought by millions until financial problems and legal woes deriving from its fraudulent health claims forced the company into bankruptcy in 1960. By the time I began working at the drugstore, its sales had dropped off considerably, and we were stuck with several unsold cases in the basement.

Some customers went directly to the shelves to get the items they wanted, but many would come to the counter and ask us for it. One product they couldn't get for themselves was condoms, which were kept in a drawer behind the soda fountain and in drawers in the back of the store. Some men were embarrassed when they came in to ask for them. I learned to joke like Calvin did by asking, "How many dozen do you want, and what size?" Some of the shyer ones would come up to the counter, look around to make sure that no one was listening, and then whisper, "Give me three."

The drugstore carried film, flashbulbs, and inexpensive cameras and provided a photo service. Customers left their exposed film with us, and every night except Sunday, David Correll, who lived a few blocks from the store, came by to deliver finished photos and pick up undeveloped film to

Hadacol, the popular tonic purported to cure almost everything. *Courtesy of thegatheringplacehomemyfastforum.org.*

take to Chapel Hill to be processed at his job in the photo department of Sutton's Drug Store.

Sometimes I helped in the pharmacy, which was located to the left of the store about three quarters of the way to the back. When I first went to work there, we poured pills into our hand and counted the correct number out into small cardboard boxes with a slide drawer like a matchbox, and then glued onto the box a label typed on an old typewriter. By the time I left the store to go off to college, we were pouring the pills into a tray, counting them with a little knife or spatula, and putting them in round plastic bottles. Many liquid medicines still had to be mixed, and Calvin even let me help with those too.

Prescriptions were numbered and then filed on coat hangers that had been straightened except for a little hook at the top so they could be hung on a nail along a wall in the pharmacy area. The very old ones, some of them going back to the early days of the store, had been moved to the basement and were still hanging there when I went off to college.

In this little town where everyone seemed to know everyone else, Warren's was far more than just a drugstore. It was also a social gathering place from morning until night. In the mornings, some women who didn't work came regularly to sit at one of the three tables and talk over a Coke or milkshake and crackers. Almost all the merchants on Clay Street came into the store daily in the morning or afternoon for a break—a soft drink and a candy bar or pack of cheese crackers—and some showed up at lunch for a prepackaged deviled egg or ham and cheese sandwich and a soft drink or milkshake. You could almost set your watch by the comings and goings. They came as much to socialize with the employees or other customers as to buy refreshments.

In the middle of the afternoon, the store was crowded with teenagers walking home from school and stopping by for a soft drink, milkshake, or ice cream cone and sitting or standing around to socialize. Many of them were my friends. We often had the television tuned to football, basketball, or baseball game on Saturday and Sunday afternoon, and we stood around watching it until a customer came in.

At night, we had a different crowd. Some people stopped by for refreshments before going to the Mebane Theater or to take a break after taking an after-dinner walk around town. Some were coming by to buy some of the grocery store–type items we carried—bottled soft drinks, potato chips, packed pints and half gallons of ice cream, candy, cigarettes, and chewing tobacco—since most of the town's grocery stores closed at 6:00 p.m. Some were coming to get prescription refills or fill new prescriptions (both clinics had evening hours). Some were coming by to get something to read—a comic book, magazine, or paperback book—or a pack of condoms in case the need arose that night on a date or at home. A series of regulars came by almost every night to have a Coca-Cola or milkshake and sit down at one of the tables and talk with one another until the 9:30 p.m. closing time.

We had some regular customers that we really didn't want. These were the drug and alcohol addicts who came in almost every day to buy products with alcohol or codeine in them. They would drink anything to get high—cough medicine, health tonics like Beef Iron and Wine, paregoric, and even canned Sterno, which was designed for camping stoves but was also swilled by desperate addicts. Federal regulations limited anyone from buying more than a few ounces per day of paregoric and codeine, but we always knew that as soon as they left our store, they went to the other two drugstores in town to round out their daily supply. Some of them became so persistent and such a nuisance that we stopped selling them the products or told them we were sold out.

In addition to serving people who came in the store, we also delivered prescriptions and other medicines to the elderly and shut-ins. I usually delivered these on my bicycle unless it was extremely cold or rainy, and sometimes the pharmacist on duty would make the delivery after the store closed in the evening.

In the summertime, we kept the door open to allow air to circulate. We had overhead fans and a big fan at the back. When business was slow on a Saturday or Sunday afternoon or evening, we would stand at the door and talk with people as they passed by on the street.

Calvin finally had air conditioning installed one summer. The difference it made was felt almost immediately. It was much more comfortable for employees and customers, ice cream didn't melt so fast when it was put on a cone or in a cup, and we didn't hear the noise of the automobile traffic passing by on the street.

But it brought other changes, too. We no longer stood in the door during slack times and talked to people as they walked by. People passed by without sticking their heads in the door to say hello or trade barbs. We now seemed more self-contained, shut off from the sights and sounds of the outside world.

Getting the job at Warren's brought a big change in my life. I was only fifteen, but at work and now at home, too, I was treated like a grown-up. I was in charge of my own comings and goings, I had a schedule to meet, and I was making my own money. I now interacted with the adult world almost—but not quite—as an equal. In my four years at the drugstore, I made my spending money and saved close to $1,000 toward college, enough for one year at the University of North Carolina.

I briefly considered going to the School of Pharmacy there, but during my senior year, I decided that I really wanted to be a college teacher. It was one of the most difficult decisions of my life, but it was the right one.

I went off to college in 1959, and in 1960, the store moved to a new building down the street on the corner across from the library and hardware store. The new store looked clean, modern, and almost antiseptic, but in my mind, it never had the character or charm of the old one.

Chapter 14
YOU CAN GO HOME AGAIN

I left Mebane in 1959 to attend college at the University of North Carolina in Chapel Hill and then to embark on a teaching career at Davidson County Community College in Lexington, North Carolina. But I still called Mebane "home" and often made the 120-mile round trip from Lexington to visit family and friends and dreamed of relocating there when Kathy and I retired.

In October 2000, we attended the "Blast from the Past," a reunion at the Arts and Community Center for anyone who ever attended or worked at Mebane School between 1903 and 1970. This nostalgic reunion was attended by over 600 alumni, teachers, and other employees and guests from across the state and nation. It was so successful that many of us returned to the Arts and Community Center in October 2003 to celebrate the 100th anniversary of the founding of Mebane School.

Over the years, I saw dramatic changes in my little hometown and the rest of Alamance County. The major drivers of these changes were the completion of Interstate 85 through the county in the late 1950s and of Interstate 40 in the 1990s, along with the closing of many furniture and textile plants as the owners moved their work to China and other foreign countries. Many downtown businesses in Mebane and Burlington shut down or relocated to the interstate corridor, and the growing population gravitated there as well. Mebane became a "tweenerville," a convenient place to live while working in the Research Triangle (Raleigh, Durham, Chapel Hill) or in the Piedmont Triad (Greensboro, High Point, Winston-Salem).

Program for "Blast from the Past." *Courtesy of the author.*

Mebane High School Class of 1959 in front of a replica of Clark's store at the "Blast from the Past." *Courtesy of the author.*

In spite of all the changes, Mebane thrived and prospered. By the turn of the century, the population had reached close to eight thousand, and by 2014, it was approaching nearly thirteen thousand. A progressive city government has successfully managed the rapid growth and provides a growing variety of services to the population. Mebane still has a fairly healthy downtown of antique shops, specialty stores, offices, and unique restaurants. Many retailers still call their customers by name and provide old-fashioned service, and during the weekdays, it's often difficult to find a parking space. Residents and visitors alike take advantage of the annual Dogwood Festival, Christmas Parade, Fourth of July Family Music Festival, Autumn Fest, and many other attractions.

Nearby Burlington was also undergoing rapid change. When Cum-Park Plaza opened on Highway 70 in Burlington in 1963, Rose's and several other Burlington stores moved there from downtown. But a bigger blow to the downtown area came in 1969, when J.C. Penney, Belk-Beck Department Store, Sears, and F.W. Woolworth left downtown for the new Holly Hill Mall that opened on Huffman Mill Road near the interstate. Then, in 2007, a large open-air shopping center, Alamance Crossing, opened by the interstate on both sides of University Drive, with dozens of stores, including Belk's, Penney's, Dillard's, Barnes & Noble, and the Carousel Cinema, a modern multiplex movie theater.

One Sunday morning in the spring of 2005, when we were visiting my sister Colleen on South Fifth Street, I decided to take a long walk through the main streets of Mebane. As I walked from her home to the intersection of Fifth Street and Highway 70, I glanced to the right at the huge White's Furniture Building, which provided jobs for so many for so long but was now mainly empty, save for a few offices that had relocated there.

I strolled up Center Street—gone, of course, were Carolina Drug Store, Coleman's clothing store, Rose's, the City Barbershop, and the Durham Bank & Trust Company. As I crossed the street, I glanced at the large mural of Mebane in 1929 painted on the side of Rice's Jewelry Story, and kept on walking past where the Mebane Theater, the post office, and Betty's Snack Shack had once been located. I turned right there, traversed the short block in front of the former Melville Chevrolet building and then cut right and ambled down Clay Street, the heart of the business district and the street I once surveyed from my vantage point as a soda jerk at Warren's Drug in the 1950s.

I stopped for a few minutes in front of the old drugstore that had been turned into a dance studio. I had always kept my connection to Warren's, stopping by to chat almost every time I visited Mebane. In 1986 I had a signing party there for my new book, *God's County: America in the Fifties*.

I crossed the street to peer through the windows of what used to be Tom's barbershop. The barber chairs and deacon's bench were gone, and the floor was littered with trash, but the little white cabinet that once held the razors, clippers, talcum powder and other tools of his trade was still there. As I stood there, it was easy to picture that little shop as it was on so many hot summer afternoons and to hear those three black gentlemen saying, "Come right in, Mr. Oakley. We'll be with you as soon as we can. How are you? How about those Dodgers?"

I passed by several buildings and then headed to my old Carr Street neighborhood. I walked down Carr Street. I used to know everybody on it, but not now. They had died or moved away. Their houses were now occupied by strangers or vacant and in disrepair. I stopped in front of the Oakley home place at 108 Carr Street. The new owners had let the bushes and flowers and small trees grow without restraint, so it had long ago lost the well-manicured look my parents always strived for. But the sidewalk my father had laid leading from the house to the road was still in excellent shape, and the completion date (10-22-47) he inscribed in the wet cement was still clearly visible.

I could barely see the front porch where we enjoyed so many hot summer evenings or the backyard where I played as a child and made so many gallons of homemade ice cream. But I could imagine walking down Carr Street from school or from a night movie or ballgame, secure in the knowledge that my parents would be there waiting for me. I could imagine the smell of burning leaves in the fall and freshly mowed grass in the summer. And even though part of it has been torn down and the remaining section is about to fall down from neglect, I can imagine Daddy standing out there in his workshop making toys for me or footstools or bookcases for the house.

As I stood there, it was easy to relive a day on that block and in that neighborhood in the 1950s. I'd come home from my paper route hungry for the sausage and eggs I knew my mother would have ready for me. Then, unless it was a school day, I'd call some of my friends to see if we could get up a baseball game that day. We'd play ball, have lunch, and then look for something else to do—perhaps play horseshoes or ride our bikes over to Second Creek or Cook's Mill and go swimming. Later in the day, we'd go by Freshwater's and sit on the front porch drinking Pepsis and eating peanuts or a candy bar. We'd then play until suppertime, and then we'd play baseball again until it was too dark to see the ball. Then it was home and to bed, and dreaming of what tomorrow would bring.

After a few minutes of longing for the good old days, I turned at the corner and continued up to Freshwater's store. It was still there, but it was abandoned and looked even more run-down than usual.

Over the years, I had often dropped by Freshwater's, the center of the neighborhood in which I grew up. I had last been in the store on October 19, 2002. As always, walking into the store early in the new millennium was like taking a trip back in time. It still looked much like it did in the 1950s. David still didn't have a telephone or bathroom, and even though it would have been very profitable, he still didn't sell beer—he had always wanted it to be a family place. It was now the town's oldest surviving business and had become something of a historic landmark. Articles about it appeared in several newspapers and magazines, and local artists had painted portraits of it that hung in many homes across town and in mine in Lexington.

David looked very tired and even older than when I had last seen him just a few months before. I told him that I was planning to write an article on the store and that I would be taking notes as we talked. After a little small talk, I asked him how long he planned to work. He shrugged his shoulders, indicating that he didn't know. He said that he would have quit years earlier if he had had a pension and been eligible for Social Security. When I asked him what would happen to the store when he quit, he said, "They'll probably bulldoze it to the ground. Then I'll sit down. I need a rest. It's been hard to take a vacation, even a weekend, for over twenty-five years." Asked what he would miss the most, he quickly replied, "My friends. The chatter, the jokes. My customers have been the best people in the world."

Sadly, he never had that time to sit down and take that rest he often talked about. Three weeks later, at the age of seventy-six, he was found dead inside the store he had worked in for so long and loved so much. It was the end of a good man and a store that had become a Mebane institution.

I sat on the store's porch for a few minutes and then walked back across town to my sister's home. It had been a good morning, a pleasant jaunt down memory lane that fortified my decision to return to the town where my life began and my heart had never left.

Finally, in 2008, Kathy and I made the difficult move to Mebane, leaving behind our friends and other associations of so many years. Alamance County has changed dramatically since those halcyon days of the 1950s that I left behind when I went off to college. But it's a great place to live—most of my family still lives in Mebane or in neighboring towns and communities in the county—and to me, it's still the "biggest little town on earth." This is where my life began, and it's where Kathy and I are enjoying renewing old friendships, making new ones, and forming new memories.

BIBLIOGRAPHY

Growing Up in Alamance County is based on my memory of living in the county in the 1940s and 1950s. The books listed below were primarily used to check my memory against some of the facts.

Books

Bamberger, Bill, and Cathy N. Davidson. *Closing: The Life and Death of an American Family.* New York: W.W. Norton & Company, 1998.

Barr, Amy Edwards, and Jerry Peterman. *Images of America: Graham.* Charleston, SC: Arcadia Publishing, 2013.

Bolden, Don. *Alamance: A County at War.* Burlington, NC: Times-News Publishing Company, 1995.

———. *Images of America: Burlington.* Charleston, SC: Arcadia Publishing, 2009.

———. *Remembering Alamance County: Tales of Railroads, Textiles and Baseball.* Charleston, SC: The History Press, 2006.

Heiferman, Marvin, and Carole Kismaric. *Growing Up with Dick and Jane.* New York: Harper Collins, 1997.

Knauff, Gail and Bob. *Fabric of a Community: The Story of Haw River.* Haw River, NC: Haw River Historical Association, 1996.

Lasley, William Kerr, Jr. *Images of America: Alamance County*. Charleston, SC: Arcadia Publishing, 1999.

Oakley, J. Ronald. *Baseball's Last Golden Age, 1946–1960: The National Pastime in a Time of Glory and Change.* Jefferson, NC: McFarland, 1996.

———. *God's Country: America in the Fifties*. New York: Dembner, 1986.

———. *Images of America: Mebane.* Charleston, SC: Arcadia Publishing, 2012.

Sink, Alice E. *Growing Up in the Piedmont Triad: Boomer Memories from Krispy Kreme to Coca-Cola Parties*. Charleston, SC: The History Press, 2012.

Troxler, Carole Watterson, and William Murray Vincent. *Shuttle and Plow: A History of Alamance County, North Carolina*. Burlington, NC: Alamance County Historical Association, 1999.

Whitaker, Walter. *Centennial History of Alamance County, 1849–1949*. Burlington, NC: Burlington Chamber of Commerce, 1949.

Yoder, Edward M., Jr. *The Night of the Old South Ball and Other Essays and Fables.* Oxford, MS: Yoknapatawpha Press, 1984.

Newspapers

Burlington Daily Times-News
Lexington Dispatch
Mebane Enterprise

Bibliography

Some sections of this book are drawn from guest columns I wrote that were published in the *Lexington Dispatch* and *Mebane Enterprise* between 1990 and 2007. The columns are listed below, and the material is used here with the permission of the newspapers.

"Christmas Is a Time for Making Memories." *Lexington Dispatch*, December 21, 2006.

"Hazel Was a Wake-Up Call for Many Tar Heels." *Lexington Dispatch*, June 7, 2007.

"It's Too Bad Paperboys Have Vanished from the U.S. Scene." *Lexington Dispatch*, October 21, 2003.

"More Plaudits for 'The Blast from the Past.'" *Mebane Enterprise*, November 15, 2000.

"Sitting on the Porch Is a Lost Tradition." *Mebane Enterprise*, November 15, 2000 (reprinted in the *Lexington Dispatch* on July 19, 2001).

"Warren's Drug Store Job Played Big Part in Man's Early Life." *Mebane Enterprise*, May 30, 2007.

ABOUT THE AUTHOR

J Ronald Oakley received bachelor's and master's degrees in history from the University of North Carolina at Chapel Hill and a doctorate in education from the University of North Carolina at Greensboro. In 2008, after teaching history at Davidson County Community College in Lexington, North Carolina, for thirty-five years, he retired to his Alamance County hometown of Mebane, North Carolina, where he has served as a member of the board of directors of the Mebane Historical Society for five years and its president for four.

Oakley is the published author of *God's Country: America in the Fifties*; *Baseball's Last Golden Age, 1946–1960*; *Davidson County Community College: The First Forty Years, 1963–2003*; *Images of America: Mebane*; and numerous articles in newspapers and other periodicals. He and his wife, Kathy, enjoy being with family, reading, participating in several book clubs, and volunteering with the Mebane Historical Society and the Friends of the Alamance County Public Libraries.